HOW TO TRAVEL
WITHOUT SEEING

ANDRÉS NEUMAN

HOW TO TRAVEL
WITHOUT SEEING

DISPATCHES FROM THE NEW LATIN AMERICA

Translated by Jeffrey Lawrence

RESTLESS BOOKS
BROOKLYN, NEW YORK

First published as *Cómo viajar sin ver* by Alfaguara, Madrid, 2010

First Restless Books paperback edition August 2016

Paperback ISBN: 978-1-63206-0-556
Library of Congress Control Number: 2016939492

Cover design by Nathan Burton
Set in Garibaldi by Tetragon, London

Printed in the United States of America

3 5 7 9 8 6 4 2

Ellison, Stavans, and Hochstein LP
232 3rd Street, Suite A111
Brooklyn, NY 11215

www.restlessbooks.com
publisher@restlessbooks.com

To the photographer Daniel Mordzinski, observer express.

To all of the friends who appear,
in camouflage, throughout this journey.

CONTENTS

Standing on this hill with no view of the sea,
I look for that very reason to the sea.

—SANTIAGO SYLVESTER

I've always had a knack for forgetting, to which
I later added a knack for walking.

—JOAN BROSSA

WELCOME ABOARD

How to Travel without Seeing

WHEN THE PUBLISHING HOUSE Alfaguara sent me the exhaustive itinerary of the book tour for their annual novel prize, I was sorry I wouldn't have more time to spend in each place. But then I thought, isn't that the point? Aren't I going to experience, without even planning it, the very essence of contemporary tourism?

*

The idea was to take notes literally on the fly. If I was going to travel by air, I would write that way, too. If I was going to spend months in airports, hotels, and way stations, the truly aesthetic thing would be to accept this situation and search for its literary side. Not to force my writing but to adapt to the times and the timetables. That way the form of the journey would be the same as the form of the journal.

*

Before I write a book, I think more about tone than about plot, listening for the book's eventual cadence. In this case I began to imagine a restless journal, told from a tight point of view and made up of a series of compact entries. One observation for each situation. One paragraph for each observation. There would never be a change of topic within a single entry. There would be no pauses. We no longer travel like that. We no longer see that way.

*

Rather than an in-depth report, I was interested in writing a cross between flash fiction, aphorism, and very short-form journalism. I would pass up the desire to recreate totalities or to give the impression of a whole. I would embrace the fragments. I would accept that traveling means, more than anything else, *not* seeing. The only thing we have is a glimmer of attention. Our small corner of happening. We wager everything, our poor knowledge of the world, in the blink of an eye. That was the interval that I chose, or that chose me, for this journey. That's why I decided that instead of taking brief notes to develop later at home, I would finish each note here and now and register discrete moments. Writing as a method of capture. A need to trap small realities on the go and interpret them in real time. Like a net that seeks to fish its own waters.

*

Of course, not having time to go into depth is a limitation for any observer. But what if that speed, that very same lightness, were also an advantage? When an exhaustive and well-documented record of a place isn't feasible, we need to rely on the poetry of the immediate, to look with the radical astonishment of the first time. With a certain degree of ignorance and thus with a certain initial hunger.

*

These days we go places without moving. Sedentary nomads, we can learn about a place and travel there in an instant. Nevertheless, or perhaps consequently, we stay at home, rooted in front of the screen. Travel in our global age is as contradictory as globalization itself. While the latter produces a tension between universal convergence and local difference, contemporary travel oscillates between the apparent pointlessness of geographical movement and the changing reality in each successive area. We always live in several places at once. Wherever we are, we can check our email and messages, read newspapers from around the world, follow international events. Wherever we go, we remain within the same landscape: the landscape of communications. That's why it seemed appealing to try writing a journal that would reflect two contradictory convictions. First, that we end up experiencing a particular world in every place we visit. Second, that through the media we spend more time in other places (or in several places simultaneously, or nowhere at all) than where we are physically. But if this is the case, then why does travel continue to transform us and teach us so much? That great *I don't know* is the subject of this book.

*

I didn't for a second want this journal to devolve into a social chronicle of the literary profession, to my mind one of the most self-absorbed and boring genres in existence. I didn't want to talk about the book tour, my novel, my personal relationships. I wanted to transcend them, to filter them through the landscape, to stretch their horizons. I only wanted to write about what I saw, heard, understood, or misinterpreted as I made my way through the labyrinth we call Latin America.

*

These days we travel without seeing anything. That's the thought that came to mind when I learned of my dizzying itinerary. The tour would be an experiment, an exaggeration of our almost empty nomadism. And on the other side of the "almost"? What would I find? What do we see when we barely see at all? What follows is my account of what I barely saw from one end of the continent to the other. An assembly of vertigos, countries, readings, glances on the fly. Latin America in transit. Are you on board?

1

The Airport, a Homeland in Transit

A DAY BEFORE TRAVELING to the real Argentina, the geographic one, I run into the invisible Argentina. At the Madrid Book Fair I meet six or seven young people with strange accents, hybrid speech. We chat for a bit. They tell me stories like my own. Listening to them, I think about the absurdity of dividing people from the same country into those living *inside* and *outside* of it. Amphibians like these kids exist and they don't detract anything from the map of their country of origin. In fact they stretch it, transplant it. We say goodbye with a strange foreign familiarity. I see them leaving one by one, children and grandchildren and great-grandchildren of Argentineans, walking slowly, both lost and finding themselves, imperfectly Spanish and incompletely Argentine, patriots of the vicissitudes of life, there in the middle of the Parque del Retiro, right at the center of nowhere.

*

An expression we often use at the airport perfectly describes the experience of migration: to be in transit. That's both how and what we are when we travel. Beings in transit. Just before embarking on a trip our sedentary side clings to stillness while our nomadic side yearns to roam. The collision of these two forces produces a sense of confusion. A certain split in our presence. That's why I revere the airport, that aseptic cathedral where passengers begin the liturgy of changing states before actually changing places. Airports are the only temples we've been able to build to the present. True shrines to terrestrial transit.

*

I'm fascinated by the introspective aspect of these constructions; they are speed merged with stillness, fortresses merged with air. Inside, our hasty lives confront an inevitable contradiction. We come to go somewhere, but we barely take a step. We want to get away, but the rhythm of the structure, its time frame and its protocols, forces us to wait. We embody that coerced patience, that urgent future that seems so distant.

*

Saying goodbye is a way of rehearsing death, but also a kind of resurrection. Airport goodbyes are both unnerving and liberating. We leave everything behind to board where everything is possible.

*

The boarding area at the Málaga airport. A flock of birds has nested in the beams and keeps crisscrossing the roof. I watch their flight from this side of the window, while on the other side the airplanes take off. These birds are like the passengers who look at them: they fly within a tiny world. Their home is the border between departure and arrival.

*

Madrid, Barajas airport, Terminal 4. "Hola, señor, hola." The woman in the indescribable suit addresses me, folder in hand: "Spaniard or foreigner?" I don't know, I answer with distracted honesty. She moves on, offended.

*

The people who shop in airports have their minds elsewhere. Their interest is self-contained; they browse without looking at what's in front of them. The people who drink coffee or eat food concentrate on some indeterminate spot floating in the distance. Others read books and enter fictional worlds, characters in hallways that are also fictions or stray paths. We all pass the time somehow, and maybe we don't pay enough attention to what a feat that is. As passengers, we make time, store it, and thus suspend the near future. On the verge of leaving, the minutes stop to examine their own condition.

*

To fly is to begin to land.

*

After taking off, our plane takes a while to stabilize. We hit turbulence as we begin to ascend. Since there's a camera installed on the outside of the aircraft, I can't help but see our swaying on the monitors: the plane looks like the Christ the Redeemer of Rio de Janeiro jumping off a cliff. I look at it—look at us—with a mixture of nervousness and disdain, as if the screen were broadcasting an accident somewhere else. Turning away, my gaze settles on the front page of today's *El País*, June 27, 2009. President Zapatero states, "The crisis has been a case of 'Land however you can.'" It's comforting to know he's already landed.

*

Zapatero speaks of the present in the past. If my plane crashed as I was writing these lines, would I be speaking posthumously about the present? Time is always in crisis. It *is* crisis.

*

I watch a couple of pretty bad movies: *City of Ember* (pseudo-science fiction film with a religious moral: the future of the world depends on us obeying Scripture and returning to our founding fathers) and *Pride and Glory* (intimate police drama also with a moral: good heroes, especially those who look like Edward Norton, will always be good). I suppose both films could be seen as models for the bicentennial epic, the independence celebrations, about to invade Latin America. I try to find consolation by reading a bit of new Argentine fiction.

*

I look over the short stories selected for the anthology *La joven guardia*, a "young guard" that is no longer so young. I read a story by Washington Cucurto that strikes me as fresh and honest (two poetic virtues) and also *machista* and badly punctuated (two national defects). I read a story by Mariana Enríquez, disturbed and disturbing: a mixture of Quiroga from Corrientes province, freaky witchcraft, and middle-class Silvina Ocampo. I find it both modern and classic. Written unpretentiously, precise and atmospheric. I read a story by Gonzalo Garcés that reflects on the very possibility of storytelling. I find it very intelligent, perhaps defensively intelligent, a characteristic quite prevalent in our university generation. The story combines a genealogical quest, Borgesian correspondences, and standard contemporary metaliterature. This last characteristic comes off as less authentic than the search for the father, or the battle with him, or both. The text shows virtuosity and a compelling sense of humor that seems not very Argentine—more English, or Catalan, or both. So what, then, is Argentine humor? To tell the truth, I don't know. But it would be violent. Less compassionate. More hierarchical. Top-down. Suddenly we land.

*

Scheherazade, Scheherazade. You became a storyteller like the others became pilots. To touch down you must have flown high.

*

They shouldn't play light music when the plane is landing. It's too much of a transcendent moment for that. Earthily mystic. Closer to symphonies or requiems. I know they play comforting music to calm passengers who are afraid of flying. But I think it's a mistake. If we were all aware of the solemnity of the landing, we wouldn't waste our time being nervous. We would simply contemplate our destiny in silence.

*

I land with part of me in other parts.

2

Buenos Aires, the Virus of the Apocalypse

I LAND AT EZEIZA AIRPORT and automatically, like someone changing the radio dial, I hear myself shift to a *porteño* accent and begin to sound like every other Buenos Aires native. I return like a foreigner to my original dialect. I switch from the firm Spanish "Buenos días" to the slippery Argentine "Buen díííaaa." Why do we greet one another with multiple days in Spain but one specific day in Argentina? Do plurinational countries communicate in the plural while centralized countries communicate in the singular?

*

We are welcomed with alien masks, cameras, and monitors that take our temperature to prevent the swine flu. All of the passengers make faces like E.T. and fill out the health forms. Next to the counter, an old sign warns of the danger of dengue fever for travelers to Bolivia or Paraguay. I think about that poem supposedly by Brecht, which in fact is neither a poem nor by Brecht, but a celebrated phrase by Father Niemöller: "And when they came for me, there was nobody left to speak for me." A few seconds later, as usual, I hesitate for a moment as the line splits: Argentineans on one side, foreigners on the other.

*

We give our names. We hand over our passports. I enter Argentina as a Spaniard. I therefore have ninety days to leave my native country. That would seem logical to me if there were a way for me to reenter Spain with an Argentine passport.

*

HOTEL IN BUENOS AIRES: Regal Pacific.
HOTEL ENVIRONMENT: Minimalism with High Roofs.
RECEPTION STYLE: Vaguely Versailles.

*

Coincidentally, I've arrived in Buenos Aires the day before congressional elections. Tomorrow the entire country votes and the dilemma is clear: either return to the dark days of Menemism through the leadership of Mauricio Macri, or stick with the progressive movement within Peronism. A vote for progressive Peronism, at this point entirely controlled by the Kirchners, means a vote against the other retrograde strains of Peronism. For better or for worse (for better *and* for worse), Argentine politics is inconceivable without Peronism.

*

I try to write "*Macrista*" on my laptop and Word corrects it to "*machista.*" AutoCorrect sometimes works like an ideology detector.

*

But what is Peronism? Any Argentinean who has tried to explain it to a curious foreigner knows how difficult the response is. For me the best explanation is this: it would be like if in Mexico the omnipresent PRI had fractured into many pieces and some ended up in power and others in the opposition.

*

The obsession with swine flu strikes Argentina. Alphabetically, the virus began its South American journey here. Just a few months ago the health minister dubbed Mexico the "sick sibling," feigning solidarity while actually maintaining her distance. Today, the debate is whether the flu should force stadiums to close next week. It's possible that the final match of the soccer championship, ironically called Torneo Clausura ("the Closing Tournament"), will have to be played behind closed doors. The strange thing is that elections are tomorrow, and voting in Argentina is mandatory. So while next Sunday the soccer stadiums could remain empty, this Sunday, the polls must be full. Many would prefer to declare the elections empty.

*

Here soccer is televised two ways: in one, you see the game; in the other, you don't. The TyC Sports cameras focus on the field, and the Fox cameras only focus on the stands. On the first channel you pay to see the players, while on the second free channel you have to settle for watching the fans at the stadium. Without access to the game itself, the TV audience follows it on their faces. They become the mirror of a game they don't see. The Argentine soccer fans have achieved an unthinkable feat: substituting for the very spectacle they are attending; getting on TV for the occasion of the game. If the citizenry could accomplish a similar feat in politics, the country would celebrate other kinds of goals. In a bar on Calle Florida, I observe the confused faces of foreign tourists, who gather around the TVs expecting to witness the event taking place off-screen. Drawn in by the sounds of the stadium, they enter the bar, order a drink, and begin to look around in perplexity. They scrutinize the other customers, trying to understand what they are viewing with such rapt attention. These invisible games make me think of Latin American forced creativity and willfulness. Would such broadcasts be successful in Europe, where many of the players I'm (not) watching now will soon be? Would TV audiences there accept such a drastic cutback? Would they settle for the shell of an image? Would they feel visually included in this exclusion? All reality is virtual until proven otherwise.

*

I read in Santiago Sylvester's poetry volume *El reloj biológico*, "Whatever is not a window is a mirror."

*

Almost all of the candidates in this election cycle have gone on the Gran Cuñado television show, a mixture of Big Brother and political puppet theater, to meet with their doubles. These were particularly honest moments in the campaign. It's the first time that professional politics has accepted its role as parody and identified explicitly with its media distortion.

*

Many of my Argentine friends hate to vote. It disappoints them. It tires them. Or they don't believe that, given the current candidates, voting is the best expression of public opinion. Maybe if soccer were mandatory and voting voluntary, the people (and soccer fans) would take voting more seriously.

*

I watch *XXY*, the first film by Lucía Puenzo, who's around my age. Based on a story by Sergio Bizzio, it's about a young hermaphrodite who can't choose between being a man or a woman. She doesn't want to decide upon an absolute identity, but rather to construct something more hybrid and ambivalent. Since this country lives in a constant state of political sensitivity, I can't help but use ideological terms to read the hermaphroditism of the protagonist—trapped between two inherited extremes that are no longer useful in explaining her world. When she tells her friend, "I pity my parents; they spend their lives hoping," I think about the utopian education of my parents' generation. When Ricardo Darín announces to his daughter, "I'll take care of you until you decide," and she responds, "What if there's nothing to decide?" I think about the elections that give so little inspiration to the country's youth.

*

The wonderful publishing house Mansalva, headed by the poet, bookseller, and musician Francisco Garamona, never aligns the margins of its pages. Due to this typographical peculiarity, in which a certain political attitude can be discerned, one reads the books with a voluble vertigo. In *Dos relatos porteños*, by Raúl Escari, I read, "I return from a bar in the Plaza Cortázar, close to my house. . . . It's called Utopía and it's open twenty-four hours. It was nine in the morning and I had gone there to drink some whiskey, something I no longer do, and . . . never should!"

*

My publisher lent me a mobile telephone (here they call it a "cell")
to stay accessible. As soon as I turn it on, I begin to receive sexually
explicit texts such as, "Hot Ass, Your Pass: text Tanga to 30303."
Should I notify the publishers? Or is it best to maintain a discreet
silence? I take the middle road and ask them, as if it's no big deal,
which writers were invited before me. As I listen to the list of fellow
writers, I take pleasure in imagining them addicted to the 30303
line. I visualize their excited faces and think: this one yes, that one
no, that one maybe. Then I realize that, come next week, I'll be on
the list of suspects.

*

Coup in Honduras. President Zelaya has been arrested. In Caracas,
Chávez criticizes the move and announces, "It's the people's hour."
I suppose that when he attempted his own coup in Venezuela, he
must have thought the same thing. Chávez refers to The People as
if it were a single unmistakable voice that, paradoxically, always
needs him as its interpreter. On TV, images of military leaders
in Honduras alternate with lines of voters in Argentina and the
Michael Jackson autopsy.

*

I don't know why, but on my day of rest I can't summon the energy
to leave the hotel, whose entrance is on Calle 25 de Mayo. Hotels
are like an empty home, and that feels liberating. "But don't hotels
seem cold to you?" my friends ask. Cold? No. On the contrary. The
street is cold: five degrees Celsius in Buenos Aires with 90 percent
humidity.

*

I walk through San Telmo. I stop in front of my childhood home, on Avenida Independencia. I peek through the black bars of the gate. I see the staircase, the porter's box, the closed elevator. Almost without thinking, I buzz up—third floor, number five. I feel a slight tremor, as though someone had pushed me from behind, and then I run away.

*

On the corner of Independencia and Defensa, a young trash collector, *un cartonero*, inspects a pile of garbage bags. He's not dressed for the cold: he wears only an Argentina national team T-shirt.

*

The *cartoneros*. Stealthy figures who take over Buenos Aires at night in order to read the city's future in papers they find in garbage bags. They deconstruct the trash, expose its inner contents. The cartoneros are not unkempt. They dress like you would if you lost your job. They also take billboard signs. They don't pay any attention to them; they simply tear them down, roll them up, and put them away. As if the paper they were accumulating had no message at all. Sly performance pieces on consumerism.

*

In a capitalist society money not only buys objects, it also sells identities. In the midst of the crisis of 2001, every corner in the city offered foreign currency. All sorts of government bonds circulated in stores. And newspapers informed bank customers how to recover the savings they'd lost, converted from dollars into devalued pesos.

All the while people didn't know who they were, on what coins they could find their faces. These faces crossed the street tensed in confusion. Now they seem calmer. But not too calm. In sync with the shadows, the light of the city has diminished in the past few years. Like a coin, Buenos Aires has two sides: one somber and the other heroic, one stuck in the past and the other forward-looking.

*

I read in *Los Lemmings*, by Fabián Casas, "The workers labor day and night to demolish the construction. Since it's made with materials from a better time, it's difficult for them to dismantle certain parts."

*

As the First World trembles, in Argentina people watch with ironic curiosity the evolution of a crisis that, for the first time, seems to hit other places worse. "You know what it is," says a taxi driver, echoing many others, "here we're already familiar with these things. We've already had the measles." What about the flu?

*

I read Samanta Schweblin's stories. Dry. Tough. Coldly observed, brutally narrated. Either without poetry or only with its skeleton. She has narrative balls that few men possess. And I'm convinced once again that her stories are among the best of our generation. They don't sound Argentine (meaning *deliberately* Argentine), or, for that matter, like they're from anywhere else. The subtlety of her realism reminds me of Guillermo Saccomanno. Her peculiarity reminds me of another writer who is actually her antipode: Hebe Uhart. In Schweblin's first book, *El núcleo del disturbio*, a dog is beaten with a stick. In her new book, *Pájaros en la boca*, a butterfly is squashed. In spite of these animal victims, or perhaps because of them, the lingering unease is starkly human. Both stories seem to tell us that without sympathy, no country can exist.

*

On election night the government is defeated in many provinces, and Néstor Kirchner loses in Buenos Aires, still the bastion of Peronism. Kirchner's candidacy was strange from the beginning (why is a former president, and one probably hoping to be president again, running for national deputy of a province where he has had little to do with?) and ended poorly. I note a vindictive and disquieting euphoria in almost all of the major media outlets. Kirchner has not been able to talk to, or at least negotiate with, the media. He was the only important candidate who didn't appear on Gran Cuñado in person. And he was also the most underperforming candidate . Which makes one think.

*

In the capital, by a margin slightly lower than predicted, the winner is Gabriela Michetti, a sensible orator and disturbing candidate of Unión-Pro, the party of Mauricio Macri. A party as artificial, para-doxical, and divided as its name, with the dash immediately after the word "union." Apparently the Buenos Aires electorate continues to dream of pizza and champagne. Macri uses my beloved Boca Juniors, a team he owns, in his campaign, and for the first time in my life I feel like a River Plate fan.

*

Pino Solanas, the filmmaker (and director of the demagogical documentary *Memoria del saqueo*, with a script that sounds like something by an Eduardo Galeano who didn't know how to write), obtains a well-earned second place in the capital. Soccer is stronger than film. Or passion defeats fiction, which requires more work.

*

I read *Vidas de muertos*, by the strange, brilliant fascist author Ignacio Anzoátegui. The book offers a sarcastic mistreatment of our national heroes. He writes of Juan Bautista Alberdi, "He said, 'To govern is to populate,' but he remained a single man." He claims of Sarmiento that "he killed culture to promote training. . . . His aspiration was for all the country's inhabitants to learn to read, even if that didn't mean anything more than reading *Crítica*," the sensationalist newspaper of the time. Anzoátegui was born in 1905, during the administrations of Quintana and Figueroa Alcorta. In other words, as Christian Ferrer explains in the prologue, he was born during a "democratic regime, a regime in which he did not believe and against which he wrote," a bit like Borges. At the beginning of the 1970s he admitted that the Argentine crisis might require an electoral solution, "only until the time arises for the country to elect a courageous, honorable and handsome dictator." Anzoátegui died in the midst of the dictatorship of Jorge Rafael Videla, who assassinated culture and imposed training.

*

I see Gabriela Michetti advancing across the platform in her wheelchair. I imagine her saying, "Argentina, rise now and walk." But the wheelchair carries her to Macri, who pushes her with one hand and waves with the other.

*

The four "leaders" of Unión-Pro speak. The first, Macri, is a pragmatic neoliberal. The second, Michetti, is a Social Democrat in foreign lands. The third, Solá, quotes Perón and addresses his union brethren in a shouting voice. The fourth, De Narváez, barely speaks the Spanish language.

*

In Jorge Fondebrider's *Los últimos tres años*, I find a poem titled "Politics": "There was a barbecue / as always, / and they talked of the same things under the vines. / But a fly knew what to do with the leftovers."

*

Many Argentineans don't say "yes." They say "obviously." The reasons are obvious.

*

I read a representative dialogue of *Savage Theories*, Pola Oloixarac's controversial, thoughtful, provocative first book. "As researchers we're very shy," the main character says, after having missed the opportunity for a couples exchange. "We aren't shy," the man replies, "this isn't the seventies." The narrator intervenes with witty impertinence: "She could admit that the guerrilla movement had infused the decade with tremendous sexual energy, but intercourse itself (and that's what we were talking about) wasn't exactly their strong suit. . . . Of course it's not the seventies; to think that promiscuity is a seventies thing is precisely what's of the seventies." "You're an idiot," she says. "I know," he agrees. "We could have had sex with them and seen what they looked like naked," she complains regretfully. "But you would have seen his dick," he says. "Who cares about his dick?" she responds, upset. "Were you afraid to fuck him because he's a man?" "I don't think he was actually a man," he whispers. "Do you want to go back?" she rejoins. "Do you love me?" he asks. "Yes. Do you love me?" she asks. "Obviously," he replies.

*

President Zelaya, now retired in Costa Rica, will return to Honduras, or at least says he will. The international community has yet to recognize the new president. What would have happened to General Videla in Argentina if the world powers, with the United States at the helm, had rejected him? Zelaya's party, by the way, does not support him.

*

At night in the hotel, after a long day, I don't check my email, I don't read books, I don't listen to music, I don't look at the news. I don't even masturbate (this really is news). Tonight, in the hotel, I watch TV while falling asleep. I watch mild, familiar, bad TV. I switch to shows from our past: *Alf, Fresh Prince, Get Smart.* And I feel, in a distant country that is also my own, in a room like any other, accidentally at home.

*

Fernanda García Lao is a writer, playwright, actor, painter, and lord knows what else. She has published the novels *Muerta de hambre* and

La perfecta otra cosa (a title that, if such a thing were possible, would sum up the meaning of life). I don't know which of the two seems more brilliant to me. Lao's life story is remarkable, and in some ways is the complementary version of mine. She was born in an Argentine province, went to school in the Spanish capital, and now lives in Buenos Aires speaking a hybrid dialect. I was born in the capital of Argentina, was educated in a Spanish province, and now try to speak like the locals in Buenos Aires, with mixed results. On her blog I find out that she works training Argentine actors to speak like Spaniards. "Argentina has become a film set for Spanish productions," I read, "and few people distinguish a *z* from an *s*. It seems simple, but it isn't." To distinguish an "underground" author from an original author also seems simple but really isn't. In Argentina there are plenty of the former. The latter, those like Lao, are scarce everywhere.

*

The obsession with antibacterial soap, retrovirals, and face masks keeps increasing. Nobody leaves home, if they leave home at all, without one of those three things. In Argentina face masks are called *barbijos*. It's strange because here they don't call the chin area *barbilla* but *mentón* or *pera*. In theory it's barbijos because of the connection with *barba*, the Spanish word for beard, but barbijos are unisex. Like viruses and fear.

*

Face masks pop up in the most remote corners of the country, and the population is divided into two. Every time a person without a mask walks by a masked person, they look at each other in mistrust. They mutually judge. They evaluate the other's condition. The masked one says, "You won't infect me, you sick animal." The one without a mask thinks at the same time, "That's not going to do you any good, you stupid alarmist." Each, in his or her own way, infects the other with the most common and dangerous virus: human nature.

*

We wash our hands. We wash our hands. After the outbreak of swine flu, we don't stop washing our hands. Finally our actions align with our principles.

*

I read *Camilo asciende*, an anthology of Hebe Uhart's short stories. Hebe Uhart is definitely weird. She has a sense of humor. She's a philosopher. She avoids photographs. She's not interested in Borges. And her name seems to come straight from "Tlön, Uqbar, Orbis Tertius." Uhart has very little in common with the major authors of her generation. It's difficult to situate her within the teleology of the national literary canon. This explains why her work has been studied so little. Although I've never had the pleasure of meeting her, I suspect that she's always been this way. As intelligent as she is discreet. Someone condemned to a generous solitude. Someone who gives the sense that she's drawing a self-portrait when she writes, "I feel so humble and genteel at the same time that I want to thank someone, but I don't know whom." Without her knowing it, I thank her.

*

The most serious political concern with respect to the flu is not Argentina's health but its economy. That is, the economic consequences that an epidemic could have in such an unstable financial environment. I walk through the fearful, wide-open streets. I think of the apocalyptic passages in *Blindness* by Saramago, *Plop* by Rafael Pinedo, *El año del desierto* by Pedro Mairal. Movie theaters, bookstores, shops, and theaters are all nearly deserted. In anticipation of an official health-alert declaration, panic deters customers. The relationship between authority and the market suddenly becomes clear: consumption depends on order.

*

On the blog of Marcelo Figueras, the author of moving novels such as *Kamchatka*, *La batalla del calentamiento*, and the recent *Aquarium*, I read, "The world sounds muffled, as if the whole country were on vacation. Every day seems like a day off. . . . The few times I go out I take taxis. The taxi drivers either don't talk or talk only about the flu. One of them tells me that he sprays the car's interior with alcohol every time a passenger gets out. After paying I get out quickly, to avoid being fumigated. . . . What comforts me about the flu, I say to myself, is that in a certain sense it's democratic. One can no longer just be suspicious of the poor. . . . But immediately I correct myself: an epidemic is democratic in its contagion, but fascist in its consequences. Those who live badly and eat worse are the only candidates for death. The well-nourished ones, like the head of Macri's cabinet, recover right away. . . . How many people die every year from the common cold . . . ? I would bet anything that more people die than have died or will die from swine flu. But . . . those who succumb to the common cold are poor people, children, the elderly, and inhabitants of remote parts of the country—the kind of people who don't look good on camera and thus don't qualify for the news. . . . I wonder if all of this isn't some reality show on a planetary scale. If I sold masks with the words 'Michael Jackson was right' I'd make tons of money."

*

Inhabitants of remote parts of the country—the kind of people who don't look good on camera. These words echo in my head as I watch *The Headless Woman*, Lucrecia Martel's latest film. This film again takes place in Salta in northern Argentina. Although it would be more precise to say that it *doesn't* take place, since everything that happens seems to form part of the protagonist's doubts. When Martel's eye focuses on the rural world, it looks extremely good on camera. That isn't to say that what we see on screen is pleasant: the north is a slow, sticky nightmare. The film doesn't belong in any way to the suspense or horror genres, a marketing fallacy that contributed to the disappointment the film met in other countries where they changed the title to *La mujer rubia* (The Blond Woman), thus losing (beheading) the element of dementia that justifies the protagonist's erratic behavior. If Martel's films did in fact have a genre, it would be rural fantasy or uncanny family drama. Class guilt and familial repression float together in these alternative portraits of the country. Rather than Argentina's politicians or her citizens, it's literature and film that decentralize the country through their fictions. Something similar could be said about the country's patriarchy.

*

I read in the poet Juana Bignozzi's *La ley tu ley*, "To buy a head of lettuce has become for me / an act of historical representation."

*

35

On the basis of Lucrecia Martel's films, we can formulate some national equations. Interior of the country = oppressed interior of the character. Outside of the country = cloudy external reality. In Argentina, the word *afuera* (outside) denominates any place beyond the country's geographical borders. But *interior* denominates any part of the country that is not the arrogant capital. Paradoxically, Buenos Aires therefore becomes a no man's land, an impossible place neither inside nor outside.

*

It rains so much in the outskirts of Buenos Aires that the car's windows are about to burst. Close to the airport it seems that every-thing—city, memory, road—is cleansed and erased, as if there had never been anything but these raindrops. These raindrops that the wind, speed without purpose, combs into the air and whisks out of my sight.

*

Sunday afternoon. The deciding match of the Torneo Clausura. It was ultimately decided that the stadium would not be closed, but the match is interrupted by another kind of alert: blocks of hail an inch in diameter are falling from the sky. Vélez and Huracán, the two teams locked in mortal combat in the championship, retreat to the locker rooms. The fans wait. The flu hushes. The sky rumbles. The rain pounds. On the empty field a ball sits in the center circle. Nobody does anything about it. Nobody but a journalist who leaps onto the playing field, skates towards the center line, lies face down and begins to take pictures. The photographer wants to capture the solitary ball, a witness to the evacuation, surrounded by hail in the middle of the field. Sitting in front of the TV in a café in the Ezeiza airport, I suddenly think that, for the sake of poetic justice, Huracán should win. Not only are they better, they also have an apocalyptic name. Someone is watching me. I'm watching the screen. On the screen, the fans are watching the photographer. The photographer is contemplating the ball. The ball is watching the enigma of this country.

3

Montevideo, Mate *in the Cathedral*

BUENOS AIRES'S AEROPARQUE. Midday. As I walk toward the ticket counter to fly to Montevideo, I realize that for the first time in my life I've forgotten my passport back in the hotel. I look through my luggage and show the employee my Spanish ID card. She shakes her head.

*

The last time I traveled to Montevideo, I was a nine-year-old boy who behaved badly for no apparent reason. We went for a club swim meet. We crossed the Río de la Plata in a catamaran. I slept in the house of a Uruguayan friend who swam faster than I did. This was in the midst of the 1986 World Cup. Coincidentally, Argentina had just eliminated Uruguay, defeating them 1-0. My friend's house had a foosball table. One afternoon, when nobody was looking, I don't know why, I bent all of the handles of the foosball table one by one. A few hours later the Uruguayan swimming club beat us badly. Not a single Argentinean beat a single Uruguayan. That night, on the eve of my return to Buenos Aires, I wet myself like a baby in my friend's bed.

*

When traveling to certain places, we move forward with our bodies and backwards in our memories. In other words, we advance into the past.

*

I fly again over the Río de la Plata. It's brown and reddish, copper and muddy. And gray. The color of history. I can't fly above these dirty waters without thinking about the Argentine airplanes that, thirty years ago, when I was still learning how to talk, threw out bodies that splashed, sunk, and disappeared. I didn't see it. I didn't know about it. It had to be told to my generation. That made us into guilty innocents. The plane turns. The clouds leave a stain on the river.

*

As I fly toward Montevideo, I start reading a story by Oliverio Coelho that, to my surprise, takes place in Montevideo. The main character, with his tired collapse and resigned love, evokes the specter of Juan Carlos Onetti's character Díaz Grey. Aside from a few rhetorical flourishes, the prose is refined, intense, and poetically physical. At this point, Onetti's (rotten) breath invigorates new Argentine fiction far more than Borges.

*

An impossible proposal for writers of the Río de la Plata: avoid the adjectives "ominous," "inveterate," and "execrable" for ten years. To write without wanting to seem *so* intelligent. How modern old Hebe Uhart suddenly seems, watering the flowerpots on her patio and crossing out words in her stories.

*

As I'm getting off the plane I run into the Argentine professor and critic Josefina Ludmer, who was on my flight without my realizing it. We say hello. I ask her about one of her former students I met a few years back. She was an interesting case. Unquestionably brilliant and perfectly bilingual because of her family, she didn't know whether to write her first novel in English or Spanish. I'm curious about her and her phantom novel. Ludmer responds that she began it in Spanish and finished it in English. *Es lo más justo*, right?

*

As soon as I get to the airport, I learn that Uruguay is about to declare a weather emergency. Another alert, I say to myself, having just left behind the health alert in Argentina. But four years ago they decided not to declare an alert, and the storm devastated half of the country since they hadn't taken the necessary precautions. What a thin line between negligence and apocalypse. An American tourist next to me vociferously demands his lost luggage.

*

I leave the airport and run into a multitude of television cameras, flashes, and microphones coming toward me. Of course, they go right on by. The soccer team Estudiantes de la Plata was also on my flight, and tomorrow they play the Uruguayan team Nacional in the Copa Libertadores.

*

According to the news, I have arrived in Montevideo during the festivities for the centenary of Onetti's birth. To do justice to the master, a funeral or a protest would be particularly appropriate.

*

I remember *The Shipyard* with hazy precision, if I may. I remember having thought after finishing it, this is what Camus would have written if he had liked adjectives.

*

Onetti's oeuvre is as lasting as human pain, sadness, and desperation. Nobody has sculpted invisible realities in Spanish as he did. Nobody has found adjectives to describe our world with such an exact evil. His work is unlike anyone else's. In life there are days, or atmospheres, or images, of which one can only think, it's as if Onetti wrote this.

*

HOTEL IN MONTEVIDEO: Tryp Montevideo.
HOTEL ENVIRONMENT: A Touch of Decay.
RECEPTION STYLE: Mistrustful of Argentineans.

*

Montevideo is the possibility of rain. Luckily the friendliness of the Montevideans means the possibility of some shelter.

*

Instead of "yes," the Uruguayans say, "It's true," "It's right." The emphasis surprises me. However, they don't say, "It's wrong" or "It's a lie." They stop at "No." Their courtesy reassures me.

*

Montevideans are *porteños* without the hysteria.

*

"Uruguay and Argentina," a friend tells me, "have leftist governments that will be defeated by the right that's now gathering its strength. Here, like in nineteenth-century Europe, there will be a Restoration."

*

On Calle Ellauri, in the wealthy or yuppie neighborhood, we go by the Punta Carretas shopping mall, which used to be an important jail. A watchtower rises at the entrance. Milling around below, shopping, are the descendants of the jailers.

*

We cross the outskirts of the city by car. "Have you seen the film *Whisky*?" the driver asks. I tell him that I have and that I thought it was excellent and depressing. "Well," says the driver pointing through the windshield, "here it is."

*

"Son of a bitch," someone says, "this cold is unbelievable!" "Winter is part of reality, man," someone else responds.

*

"I returned from Buenos Aires to Montevideo," writes the poet Daniel Viglione, "to find out what my first kiss would have been like on Montevideo's boardwalk, with this insufferable wind."

*

One in the morning, hotel TV. "Mr. Attorney General of Honduras," the CNN reporter asks, "if President Zelaya truly broke the law, why didn't you take legal action, instead of also breaking the law to depose him?" "Miss," answers the attorney general, "you have to live in this country to understand." And unwittingly, the attorney general summarized the whole history of Latin America in just ten words.

*

During the dictatorship, members of the Tupamaro guerrilla group were held in the Punta Carretas prison. Some managed to escape. One of them was Pepe Mujica, currently a Uruguayan senator and the leading candidate for the presidency. Later the Tupamaros were imprisoned again. And tortured, I imagine. I go into the shopping jail. I cross the main arch and read, "Delicacies all day every day." I cross the patio and read, "July 12th, Father's Day." In the background looms the Sheraton Hotel.

*

The former prison is pleasant, disturbingly pleasant. Pastel tones, relaxing music, well-lit window displays, sleek escalators. There are shops everywhere, tables with soft drinks, ATM machines. Inmates dig tunnels.

*

I leave the building and, as if transported to the 1970s, a girl hands me a flyer and then disappears. The flyer says, "Travel to the stars by savoring the new Whopper Trek."

*

I read *Disco duro*, a collection of articles by the fearsome and entertaining writer Gustavo Escanlar. In one of them, an inspector receives the assignment of examining why Eduardo Galeano is so popular. Although the pay is good, another inspector tries to dissuade him from this dangerous mission. "Don't mess with Galeano," he counsels, "he has friends in high places." "In government?" the protagonist asks. "No . . . even higher," the other responds, "he's friends with the gods." But the protagonist isn't deterred and inquires which books he should get to begin his investigation. "Look," the other answers, "the most famous is *Open Veins of Latin America*. But nobody—literally nobody—has read the whole thing. I'll summarize it in a single phrase: Everything is the colonizer's fault." The inspector begins to deduce that the author's work comforts Latin Americans, who are happy to be good, just as much as it comforts Europeans, who feel guilty about being bad. In his final report, the inspector concludes, "Galeano is a religion: appealing to the readers' faith, he tells them what they need to hear. Faith is more important than truth. That's why Galeano is more often invoked than read. Like the Bible or the Koran."

*

Facing Plaza Primero de Mayo, ugly and soulless in its homage to the workers, is the Legislative Palace, home to the Senate and House of Representatives. We try to visit the Hall of Lost Steps, the famous room that seems to cite Alejo Carpentier and Andrés Trapiello. We are denied access. We must ask for authorization in the Protocol Office. We go to the Protocol Office. There we are told there are no visits except during official visiting hours. "When you enter without asking," my companion explains, "nobody stops you." But we asked. And that was our error in the Legislative Palace, the symbol of democracy. I will never set foot in the Hall of Lost Steps.

*

I recall Uruguayan books, and also some films, where bureaucracy is elevated to the category of perception. There seems to be something very Montevidean about the attention to slowness, to the profound mystery of inefficiency. In a story by Pablo Casacuberta, I read, "At the entrance to the office, under the threshold, a woman sits waiting for the resolution to a case that is urgent for her and clearly not so for the person in charge. I've watched him stare at her for more than twenty minutes, like a professional con man, and then tell her to come back in a second." A great amount of the country's literature takes place during that infinite second. Maybe this temporal equation explains why its stories so often give the impression that nothing happens and nonetheless communicate such intensity, such uncertainty.

*

On the wall of the Artigas Institute of Professors, I read the graffiti, "Because the dead are the ones who should be alive, and the assassins are the quick and the living."

*

We get into a taxi. The driver argues with the car attendant, who helps people park in exchange for a tip. "Don't get involved," the taxi driver scolds. "I don't need anything from you," says the attendant. When the door closes, the taxi driver calms down and sighs: "Finally. In the words of George Bush, let there be peace!"

*

The cathedral in Montevideo. At the entrance: "No *mate* allowed in the temple."

*

A photo session inside the cathedral. While people pray in silence, the photographer's flash emits strident noises. Two different ways of searching for the light.

*

The airport in Montevideo. I realize that I arrived too early. I kill time reading Mario Levrero. Or better yet, I relive time by reading him. Soon I'll be flying over the dirty Río de la Plata once again. But this time I didn't wet anyone's bed. Consider it an improvement.

*

Levrero's posthumous work, *La novela luminosa*, is not actually a novel, though that doesn't really matter. As luminous as it is voluminous, written in the early mornings, the entire book speaks of the desire to write. Or the lack thereof. Or the need to write in spite of everything. Light, the desk lamp that's on at all hours, is that need. The writing never really happens, and this inconclusiveness paradoxically allows for its development. From the many passages I was prompted by the author's reflexive obsession to underline, I copy one that explains his theory of trains and synthesizes the journey of life and the life of journeying: "One constantly takes trains that go to different places and travel at different speeds—and one takes these trains at the same time, and sometimes trains that go in opposite directions. . . . It's a giant movable train station, from which trains are constantly leaving that will or will not arrive at their destination, that will or will not return to the station, each one carrying a small anxious 'me', with its yellowish face glued to the window, eyes wide open. . . . To know how to coordinate the movement of the trains in their entirety is the art of writing, just as the art of living is to know how to coordinate them in real life. I am ignorant of this latter art to a frightful degree. I hope, on the other hand, though I don't count on it, that the literary art will give me some recompense. Thus I begin this chapter with renewed . . . " Suddenly we are asked to board.

4

Santiago, the Self-Absorbed Order

AEROLÍNEAS ARGENTINAS. Flight 1288. Destination: Santiago, Chile. After seeing hand-sanitizer dispensers crop up all around me, I decide to wash my hands one more time. I go into the restroom, but I don't see any soap. I ask the stewardess where they keep it. She shrugs her shoulders. So you don't have soap? I persist, incredulous. "Of course we do," she answers, "but it's the kind you have to screw in and it doesn't fit. The soap bag is bigger than the thing in the sink. Okay? That's why it doesn't fit." Oh, I cautiously reply. So will you give me some? She hesitates: "I'm not sure we have any." I suddenly remember the jingle the company played on TV ads when I was a kid: *Aerolíneas Ar-gen-tiii-naas! Argentina soars through the skies.*

*

The first thing that strikes me about Chile, before arriving in Chile, is the customs form. It's not like the others. It seems designed to confirm the image of Chile abroad: professionalism, progress, legality, order. It's clearer than the Argentine form, which is long and redundant. It's also better than the form for Spain. The Chilean sheet is brief and reasonable. Modern, with large print and wide spacing. It has a certain ostentation, a sense of whitewashing, of "nothing wrong here." Can one make comparisons between countries based on their customs forms, like one does with newspapers? "We now have soap," the stewardess informs me.

*

"I left my backpack under there," says a young kid with huge headphones around his head. "Huh? What? Sorry?" an old man answers crossly. The kid looks at him in frustration, takes off his headphones, and repeats the phrase. "Oh, okay." The man smiles, satisfied, and moves his things from the seat to free up the kid's backpack. Then we set foot in Chile.

*

The greatest source of contagion in our day is conversation. In Santiago everyone's talking—surprise, surprise—about the financial crisis and swine flu. Did the plane actually get off the ground? I ask myself whether going somewhere and traveling are the same thing.

*

HOTEL IN SANTIAGO: NH Providencia.
HOTEL ENVIRONMENT: Very Spanish High Standard.
RECEPTION STYLE: Slightly Ironic Courtesy.

*

Pijo, concheto, fresa, pituco, cuico . . . Like other countries, Chile has many words to name this reality. Our language is one, multiple, global. Like classism.

*

Surrounded, protected, separated by the beauty of the mountain range, a bit like my Granada, Santiago is engrossed with itself.

*

A certain impenetrability, a defense from something that's hard to pinpoint.

*

Port cities contemplate visitors with ancestral understanding. From the beginning of time, foreigners have come to do business. That's why in maritime cities people look at us as if to say: What would you like? Whereas in mountainous cities (particularly those surrounded by mountain ranges) people look at the visitor with ancestral suspicion. From the beginning of time, foreigners have only come to invade them. That's why people look at us here as if to say: What are you doing here? Nobody summons the energy to cross the Andes with good intentions. Except our national hero San Martín, who ended up in exile.

*

"When Bolaño visited Santiago, he seemed like a jerk to me." This opinion is often repeated in private within the local literary milieu. In Chile, as strange as it might sound, Bolaño appears to be much more discussed than read. As if in death he continued to stand between his masterpieces and readers in his homeland.

*

Montevideo: "People will love the novel here." Santiago: "It probably won't sell here." Buenos Aires: "You explained the book well."

*

"It's not a coup," the new authorities in Honduras declare. "It's simply that Parliament has deposed the president and the Army executed that order."

*

I don't know why, but when I walk the streets of Santiago I imagine Bolaño laughing at me.

*

Early in the morning, I am notified that my interview with *La Segunda* has been canceled. Why? "The journalist is no longer there." At the place where we're supposed to interview? "No, at the paper."

*

In Chile the soccer championship season is also ending, though here it's the Opening rather than the Closing Tournament. The final match between Universidad Católica and Unión Española will determine the title. Unexpectedly, the match here is also in danger of being canceled. Not because of swine flu, but because a neighbor has tried to legally block the match. Apparently, every time an important match is played in the Santa Laura stadium, there are acts of vandalism in a school nearby. "The only thing the fans of the different teams have done," stated the brave school principal, who today became public enemy number one for the most savage fans, "is destroy and rob this institution." The media is giving broad coverage to the case, but nobody seems particularly interested in condemning the destruction or demanding greater security for the school. They also don't appear to have thought about protecting the identity of the accuser, who has presented an appeal to the appellate court to move the match to another stadium. The city and local government of Santiago had already given their approval for the match.

*

I notice that the trend here is to photograph writers with a low-angle shot, forcing them to look at the reader who observes them from above. Does this mean anything?

*

I flip through back issues of the culture section of the newspaper. I have fun comparing the articles with Argentine ones. If the predominant tone in Argentina is learned exhibitionism, in Chile the norm seems to be grumpy aggression. Some of the articles seem intended to demonstrate that the critic is much more intelligent than the author. Others, to dissuade the publishing house from distributing more books by the author in the country. Between lessons and expulsions, there is little room for pleasure.

*

"At the university," she tells me, "my philosophy professor raised our grades for going to the marches against abortion." At first I think she's being ironic or hyperbolic, but she keeps looking at me with complete seriousness. And continues, "Many Chilean men think abortion is taboo. They don't even consider it. Our wombs belong to them." I nod. I'm thinking. And I hold back a politically incorrect thought: In Spain the exact opposite thing tends to happen. There the womb belongs to women (as it should), but so does the child. And the man who has engendered it often has no right to participate in the decision of what to do with it. It's not as horrible as the reverse, but it also seems to me to be a problem. Especially if we want fathers to be as responsible for their children as mothers.

*

We don't travel by looking, but by listening.

*

"Those of us who were young when Bolaño's books arrived in Chile," someone tells me, "were struck, illuminated by him. But those who were not so young had the opposite reaction." It makes sense. It's not the same to be struck as it is to be run over. Being illuminated is not the same as being eclipsed.

*

"Crossing the Andes to get to the sea," says my friend. I don't know if that feat is utopian, or atrocious, or both at the same time.

*

Chileans speak in solitude. Argentineans speak to themselves.

*

A Jorge Teillier poem says the following: "A whisper—for whom? / between one darkness and another."

*

Here people look at the mountains peacefully. Confronted with the colossal, mitigation and ambiguity.

*

Bolaño was a Chilean who wrote the great Mexican novel while living in Catalonia. Nevertheless, he was rabidly Latin American. He found a way to become Mexican, couldn't help being Chilean, and was often amused by the idea of disguising himself as an Argentinean. Bolaño was Pan-American, but now we're seeing a change. Many young writers are trying to stop being the symbolic property of their countries. Not to be from other countries, but to not be from any.

*

In a Peruvian restaurant in Santiago, I order a *Causa colonial* and a sea bass *a lo Macho*. I'm tempted to raise a glass to La Malinche and to Oscar Wilde.

*

Bolaño voiceless from living. Bolaño dying from laughter, dead.

*

In a poem by Óscar Hahn, I read, "Rise and go to the hospital said the voice / I'm the ghost from before you were born / It's still not time for the other ghost / Your death will profoundly affect you / You can never recover from your death."

*

I have no idea whether Nicanor Parra, the greatest Chilean poet of his era, likes to chat on the phone. But, if his poetry is any indication, I'm almost certain that Parra is a conversationalist. I recall these lines of his: "I hopelessly fell into the trap of the telephone / which attracts everything around it like an abyss." Bolaño, a compulsive phone talker, greatly admired Parra and imitated him. Not only in his poems, but also in his mysterious dialogues. I reread Parra's "The Two Friends," and I imagine both authors suddenly meeting in some impossible place, running into each other and saying, "Good morning, Juancho, my friend / Good morning, Lucho, my friend / Where are you going, my friend / on such a rough day. / What do you mean rough, my friend: to the capital of Rome. / The capital of Rome? / The Capital of Rome! / The ways of my friend! . . . / The Pope doesn't believe in God / What do you mean he doesn't believe in God! / The Pope doesn't believe in anything. / I know he doesn't believe in anything / The ways of my friend! / I'm sorry, Juancho, my friend. / I know you don't believe in anything. / Can I ask you something? / Ask away, my friend. . . . / Seriously, Juancho, my friend / what do you get by going to Rome! / What do I get by going to Rome? / You know what I've always liked: / Ever since I was born I've always trailed / after eternal life. . . . / After eternal life. / Don't make me laugh, my friend. / Don't you see how angry you got? / You know what, my friend / things become clear by talking: / I'll buy you a drink."

*

I read on the front page of *El Mercurio* in Chile, "Theaters Closed in Buenos Aires to Prevent Spread of Flu." Alarmed, I open the paper to find the article and discover an important clarification: the president of the Argentine Association of Theater Businesses has stated that the suspension (for just ten days) is not because the "epidemic has gotten worse, but because so few people are going to the shows." From the headline to the actual news article there is a world of difference: from a health apocalypse to simple economic pragmatism.

*

We discuss Alonso de Ercilla's *La Araucana* and its borderland discourse. The story of a conqueror who can't avoid becoming fascinated with the conquered characters. We talk about how this long poem has been used as a patriotic testimony on both sides: the great epic of the Spanish Conquest; the heroic indigenous resistance. At that exact moment, we hear a news story on the taxi's radio that leaves us in silence. When I get back to the hotel, I search for the story in different sources to guarantee a certain neutrality. I read: "Today the Carabineros, the national police, prevented a group of one hundred *lonkos*, or political chiefs, from the Mapuche communities that live in the south of Chile, from presenting a letter with demands for their ancestral lands to the Chilean president, Michelle Bachelet. . . . 'We submitted the letter to show that we are open to dialogue, so they won't again accuse the Mapuche people of committing terrorist acts,' maintained one of the community's messengers, known as a *werken*. In a statement, the indigenous people indicated they did not have a scheduled meeting with the president, and they explained that they tried to make an appointment through the municipal government of Araucanía, in the south of the country, but that they received 'no response.' For its part, the municipal government of the region acknowledged in another statement that 'the commission of the Mapuche territory submitted letters to schedule a meeting with the president,' but according to the authorities, 'they refused to leave a postal address to respond, leaving only telephone numbers at which they never answered. . . . ' Among the Mapuche representatives that came today was Edmundo Lemún, the father of young Álex Lemún, who died in 2002 after being shot in the town of Ercilla, presumably by a police officer. . . . The Interior Minister, Edmundo Pérez Yoma, denied any police repression in the area. 'That is absolutely untrue; the situation in these parts of Araucanía is a situation we can define as normal,' he assured."

*

In *Trama y urdimbre*, a micronovel by Matías Celedón, I read, "He had forgiven him in writing. The man did not acknowledge receipt."

*

We visit the Plaza de Armas. The cathedral of Santiago is gorgeous. There are a number of Peruvians sitting on the edges of the structure. Not only on the edges of divine law but also of human law. They are, O Latin American brethren committed to resistance against the imperial invader, illegal immigrants. A small handwritten sign announces, "Thursday the 9th, Concentración Catedral, 10:00 a.m. Migrant march to La Moneda for ID cards." On the other side of the same sign, it reads, "Enough abuse!! Thursday the 9th, 10:30 a.m. March to La Moneda for immediate permanent residency certificates!!" Tragically, the times for the march don't coincide.

*

When the same thing that's happening to these Peruvians happens to a Latin American in Spain, the children of Bolívar, San Martín, and Artigas raise an angry cry to the heavens. I don't know if Father Hurtado, the defender of the poor and homeless whose statue adorns the cathedral, would have done something about this situation. His successors, if they existed, evidently didn't. O ye children of God, some more than others.

*

In a poem by Francisco Véjar, I read, "Ruins, so deep / that even time cannot destroy us."

*

Taxi from the cathedral to the Providencia neighborhood (which is not without its logic). We stop and the taxi driver takes a long time printing the receipt. "It's like baked bread," he explains to us. "It takes a long time, but eventually it comes out."

*

When I woke up, the mountain range was still far away.

*

"Sorry to bother you," says the driver who takes me to the airport, "but this writing business, does it come from one's parents? What do you think? I'm asking because my daughter writes. By herself. She tells stories. By herself. We bought her a computer. A 1998 model. Outdated, right? But she writes on it. Her mother and I can't read."

*

In *The Private Life of Trees*, Alejandro Zambra's most recent novel, everything waits: the plot, the character, the prose. Godot taught us that the ones we wait for almost never come. From that post-modern certainty, which in someone else's hands could lead to a disappointment, comes the dilation, the reflection, the ambiguity of this novel. Nothing happens and we learn so much. Or, to put it another way, everything is possible because nothing happens, and in the meantime, the character waits. Zero action, maximum tremors. These are Zambra's worlds. Minute and strange intimacies. Something very fragile within something that seems at peace. I'm not sure how much of Chile there is in all of this.

*

Santiago Airport. TAM Airlines ticket counter, Flight 709 to Asunción, Paraguay. The employee, a very beautiful brunette who went by no other name than Claudia Ximena Mondaca Pinina, asks me, "Can you give me a number?" "What?" I ask, hopeful. "Yes," Claudia Ximena Mondaca Pinina explains, "we need the number of someone who is not traveling with you, in case we need to notify them." I swallow. She smiles. With pity.

*

Airport store. Book section. I see an English edition of *Cathedral of the Sea*, by Ildefonso (*Illdeefóunsou*) Falcones. Best sellers. Self-help. Detective novels. There are also other things: contemporary Chilean literature (Lemebel, Costamagna, Fuguet), various anthologies of Gabriela Mistral and Pablo Neruda. The latter might seem obvious since we are in Chile. But, honestly, I can't remember a single Spanish airport where they sell poetry compilations by Lorca, Juan Ramón Jiménez, or Vicente Aleixandre (who was also a Nobel Prize winner). Tonight I can write the saddest entries.

5

Asunción, Holes and Questions

TAKE-OFF ON THE FLIGHT from Santiago to Asunción. A stewardess roams the aisle spraying us with disinfectant. She moves slowly, fumigating us with a twirl of the wrist, looking the other way. It seems like she's holding her breath the entire time. Aerial cockroaches, we passengers look at her solemnly, safe from our own plague.

*

As the plane taxis down the runway and our sleepiness begins to take off, a metallic voice welcomes us aboard the flight with a final destination of Santiago. My eyes shoot open in panic. I look around. What terrible mistake have I made? Did I take the wrong plane? Where am I now? And where were we before? Didn't we just *leave* Santiago? Is time circular? Has space collapsed? Is there another dimension? Am I two people at once? Are all places the same? Beside me a passenger laughs, points to the speaker, and shakes his head.

*

"But, Mom, why are we above the sky?" a girl asks.

*

The inevitable, crushing humidity: we have arrived in Asunción.

*

"The most beautiful thing in Paraguay is Paraguay," a tourist flyer reasons. This makes sense, considering I just flew from Santiago to Santiago.

*

Something has changed definitively. At the immigration counter, I see the first electric fan of the entire trip.

*

HOTEL IN ASUNCIÓN: Las Margaritas.
HOTEL ENVIRONMENT: Luxury à la Tropicale.
RECEPTION STYLE: Between Suave and Hermetic.

*

In Paraguay more than half the population is bilingual, and at least half of those who speak Guaraní consider it their mother tongue. This is indeed a difference in the landscape.

*

The first version of *Don Quixote* was just published in this watery tongue. "It's not a translation," they explain, "but an adaptation. The novel is in rhymed verse and it's narrated by a speaking voice. It sounds like Hernández's *Martín Fierro* in Guaraní." Without even reading it, I already love it. The idea is straight out of César Aira.

*

I ask if there are novels written in Guaraní, and I'm told there aren't; because of the orality of the language, the majority of works are poems or the retelling of traditional stories. I ask if anyone describes the urban reality of Asunción in Guaraní. I'm told that that's the function of *jopará*, a mixture of Guaraní and Spanish used primarily for dialogue. Or *portuñol*, the Spanish-Portuguese blend typical of the border area with Brazil. I find it strange I've never read anything about these experiments in hybridity, and it surprises me that these complex linguistic phenomena are not more widely studied, because in other countries, in other border areas, they capture the attention of scholars and the media. "Welcome to Paraguay. That's how it is here," or *Así es acá*. In Guaraní, by the way, *Akã* means "head." Which is what we should use more often in order to wrap our minds around certain countries.

*

At night we speak to each other, we look at each other on Skype, we make love via video chat. Or rather, we don't. We masturbate together, separately. Where are each of us? In what country? Distance is shortened and at the same time becomes palpable; we feel closer and yet further apart. We don't orgasm at the same time. It makes sense: the signal is delayed.

*

The messages intended for others seem to pursue me. When I wake up I turn on the local cell phone loaned to me by the publishers and read, "Dedicate three works to God and your dreams will come true." Seen from my hotel room, the Paraguay River seems like an atheist.

*

"Welcome to Asunción," says the driver, "the pothole capital of the world."

*

We drive along Calle Mariscal López. Um. Wait a second. Marshall López. A vague recollection from my school days flickers like a flashlight with low batteries. Wasn't that the guy who exterminated his people by entering a war against the Triple Alliance? No less than Argentina, Brazil, and Uruguay, with a little help from the UK? The very one, the very one. "But he continues," they tell me, "to have both supporters and detractors." And the supporters, I ask, what do they say? "That he was a leader," they respond. The car turns off Calle Mariscal López and we start down another street.

*

In José Pérez Reyes's story "The Burier of Portraits," I read, "I can't stand people who decorate their houses like a pantheon. That bad habit of hanging old pictures makes the place even more depressing. . . . As far as I'm concerned, they can put their epoch somewhere else. I don't want them invading the present. My only defense is vengeance."

*

I tell my editor that I received a message this morning to get in touch with God. "Lucky for you," she says.

*

The sharp Paraguayan sigh.

*

When I arrive at Channel 13, I'm offered coffee in the waiting room, which also doubles as the bathroom and makeup room. I drink my coffee and give the cup back to the woman who served it. She slowly nods her head, disappears for a few seconds, and returns with the same cup still dripping with water, which she places on the dusty table from which she had taken it to serve me. Reaching me from the monitor, the announcer speaks in a monotonous voice about the flu contagion.

*

"Did you kill her?" shouts the journalist from Channel 13. "Negative," responds the accused man.

*

The newspaper *Última Hora*. Their modest slogan: "Read the truth."

*

At least one article in *Última Hora* seems to validate the slogan. Today's paper, July 9, Argentine Independence Day, or not so much. I read that Paraguay's Ministry of Public Health buys antivirals for 8,500 guaraníes (around $1.70), while the drugstores in the country sell them for 148,000 guaraníes (almost $30.00). In other words, customers pay seventeen (seventeen!) times the cost of the pills to fight the flu. I wonder if this epidemic isn't just one big marketing campaign, engineered to combine the real panic in the world with the resources of an apocalyptic blockbuster. That formula has a guarantee of success at the ticket booths. Of the drugstores. Meanwhile, I begin to sneeze.

*

In the department of San Pedro, in the eastern central zone of Paraguay, Nietzsche's sister wanted to found New Germania, a delirious utopia of Aryan purity. The experiment was a glorious failure: today there are mestizos who speak German and Guaraní.

*

I spend my free day in Areguá, twenty miles from Asunción. Several wealthy artists live, or have taken refuge, in this beautiful town. This is also where Gabriel Casaccia's *La babosa*, a foundational novel of Paraguayan literature, is set. Areguá reminds me of the Argentine province Misiones: its meditative subtropical rainforest, its dreamlike fog, the violent contrasts of the blood-red land. We go to lunch at the home of the artist, architect, and writer Carlos Colombino. I had been warned that the place was unusual, but the actual sight of it was beyond my wildest imaginings: an injection of Bauhaus in the midst of the jungle, a floating convent ripped away by a typhoon, a cubist deconstruction of Horacio Quiroga. The vast main room, which you access through a ramp, serves up a spectacular view of Lake Ypacaraí. On the lower floor, there is an atelier and a bedroom with a door the shape of a trapeze. The entire building is an incredible polyhedron without walls, a concrete structure traversed by windows. The owner explains, "The elements penetrate ferociously into the house: light, rain, sun, lightning. I built it like this so I wouldn't have anywhere to hide."

*

In addition to being a notable writer, Carlos Colombino is also a benefactor of Paraguayan art. He founded the stunning Museo del

Barro, where indigenous pieces cohabitate with avant-garde works from the Hispanic world. Cosmopolitan and gay, sarcastically cultured, his life has run parallel to the bloody history of Paraguay: its dictatorships, persecutions, and homophobias. Colombino speaks of his country with a humor covered in scars. He calls it the "horrific nest." Or the "island surrounded by silence." Or, citing Roa Bastos, the "country enamored with misfortune."

*

"How horrible," sighs Colombino, "how time flies, and how the great son of a bitch enjoys himself."

*

"I wanted to show time," explains Paz Encina. I just borrowed *Paraguayan Hammock*, the director's first film and the first film I see in Guaraní. It's a story that develops internally. It takes place in the interior of Paraguay: within its territorial heartland, its memory, its language. And in the interior of its characters. Overwhelmed by the heat, a rural couple waits, or has stopped waiting, for the return of a son who went to war. The son never arrives. And neither does the rain. The background is the bloody Chaco War, unleashed between two poor countries without a coastline. After the end of the war, an endless period of dictatorships began in Paraguay. Bolivia did not fare any better. Only recently, seventy-five years after that war, have the presidents signed a definitive accord regarding the border. Motionless as the hammock where the old couple converse, the film expounds on the emptiness of the daily routine when a loved one has been lost. The camera refuses to invade the characters, to interrupt their mourning. All we hear, in the distance, is a dialogue between ghosts. And the sounds of the countryside. Nothing more. Nothing less. "I hear the birds," he says, "but I can't see them." A story about waiting that matures into desperation, his wife describes it like this: "There's no way to fight what doesn't come." And, although it's not a film about collective discourse, the entire country agrees.

*

"Who cares about us?" a friend submits. "If at this very moment an atomic bomb fell on Paraguay, nobody would even notice. We don't have any influence in the world." His wife corrects him: "Why do you want to have influence in the world? It's much better to go unnoticed."

*

I read on the cover of the newspaper *ABC Color*, "Brazil wants to finance a census of Brasiguayans. The degree of hostility against Brazilians and their descendants in Paraguay is a major source of concern in the neighboring country."

*

Asunción airport. Waiting room of the Brazilian airline TAM. I notice a small sign addressed to employees, with the seven commandments of the company's CEO. They could be used as the neoliberal pirate's Bible of our age. Here are four of them: *1. Nothing replaces profit. 3. Security is more important than the customer. 4. The easiest way to make money is not to lose it. 7. He who lacks the intelligence to create must have the courage to copy.* But when I go onto the airline's website, I find a section with the company philosophy: "First rule: the customer is always right. Second rule: if the customer is ever wrong, reread the first rule." At the bottom of the sign in the waiting room appear the CEO's signature and photo. Clearly he's dying of laughter.

*

PEMBOTY OKẼ
(Please close the door)

6

La Paz, How to Climb History

TO FLY FROM ASUNCIÓN TO LA PAZ, which is less than two thousand miles away, I first have to go from Asunción to Cochabamba, where the plane makes a stop, and then from Cochabamba to Santa Cruz. There I have to wait four hours and change planes before arriving in La Paz. If there were any justice in this world, all Bolivian passengers would have platinum cards.

*

Over the past few days I've repeatedly been warned, threatened almost, about the altitude in La Paz, a place I've never been. According to popular wisdom, this city at two and a half miles has three important "little" things. That is, you eat little, you walk little, and you sleep by your little self. I hope it's a myth.

*

From the window I see San Pedro Hill with the enormous Christ atop, feet rooted to the land of his minuscule servants, arms wide open, envying the planes.

*

I land in Santa Cruz. I've been in this airport before, but I barely remember anything. We travel without a past, we erase while we travel, we fly while we forget. A traveler is a mixture of moving amnesia and fleeing memories.

*

I walk to the ticket counter of Aerosur to ask for my boarding pass. The agent says, "But that flight is not till tonight!" I ask if he can give me the boarding pass now. "Later," he responds, "we have a meeting now." And suddenly the airline's ticket counter is deserted.

*

Two details capture the essence of the airport: there are no escalators and there are shoe-shining stalls.

*

We finally begin our descent, or ascent, into La Paz. Our plane will climb up up and away, to the summit that is the airport. I wonder if, how, how much the altitude will affect me. My preparation has been awful: Santa Cruz is at sea level and Asunción 650 feet above it. I don't know if I'm afraid, curious, or both. I suddenly think of the Argentine national team, which was crushed by the Bolivian team 6-1 in La Paz.

*

Bathe in an infusion of coca leaves. That's it.

*

Despite the dizziness, I quickly notice an oral particularity: here the poorer people speak in chiasmus, concluding with the same phrases with which they begin. They loiter around the idea, formulate it, and prudently return to where they started. Like someone who decides at the last moment to run to safety.

*

I have arrived right during the bicentennial celebrations: Bolivia became independent two hundred years ago on July 16. There are many events scheduled and multicolored lights hang on all the streets. On the promenade known as El Prado, but actually named July 16, there is a statue of Columbus. He is perched atop his pedestal, still surveying his discovery. "With all due respect, señor," the driver explains, "that statue is unpopular here, many people want to take it down, that Spaniard—" It's not really known, I interrupt, whether he was Spanish. "Fine, that may be true, but he came with the Spanish, right? And people say that he should leave once and for all, that Bolivia is ours, you see? With all due respect, señor." I'm about to say, but I don't dare, that he's talking about something that happened half a millennium ago. That precisely because they are celebrating two hundred years of independence, it's about time for them to take responsibility for the situation in the country and their own politicians. That it was the Bolivian oligarchy, and not Columbus, that monopolized the resources and screwed the indigenous people for two hundred years. And that that's why, in all fairness, Evo Morales won.

*

"Here there are many ignorant people," the driver explains. "We now have an indigenous president, you know. Here there are many ignorant people; someone says something and they do it, señor." I nod. I look at him; he has indigenous features. I don't know if his words are a criticism of the government, a courtesy to the white passenger and the Spanish company that pays him, or a totally ironic statement. I realize that the strength of the Bolivian character resides in that ambiguity.

*

HOTEL IN LA PAZ: Plaza.
HOTEL ENVIRONMENT: Formerly Modern.
RECEPTION STYLE: Elliptical.

*

The altitude affects me less than I had anticipated. I feel only a slight strangeness while breathing, as if my chest were made of a fragile material. I walk cautiously and feel pretty good. They tell me that, just in case, I should take sorojchipills. Sor what? I respond quizzically. Sorojchi pills. In Aymara, *sorojchi* means altitude sickness. Everything else is capitalism.

*

From my room, the nighttime view of the mountains and its infinite lights overwhelms me. This city is not between mountains, but *in* the mountains, *on* them. A metaphor of its own History, the Bolivian capital has grown by scaling itself, building an uphill destiny for itself.

*

Every day that goes by, I'm not sure why, I feel more and more retrospective interest for the deceased Michael Jackson. It's as if his role as victim were only believable now that he's no longer here, now that he can't complain, now that he can no longer make the face of a mistreated child who sleeps with children. A hypercommercial artist who was capable of inventing, of innovating in more than one sense. I regret having underestimated that ability. I walk by a stand with pirated discs (in Bolivia, piracy is the main national industry), and, almost without thinking, I select a DVD. It's the first time I buy a pirated disc, and the first time I buy something by Michael Jackson. *Bad*, the 1987 tour, Tokyo. The dead man, live.

*

The obelisk in La Paz seems like a stylized version of the one in Buenos Aires, which is bigger, dirtier, and more phallic. Next to the obelisk sits the monument to the unknown soldier, a memorial to the Chaco War. I contemplate the figure of the facedown soldier, closer to a sleeping boy than a bullet-ridden corpse. On the plaque I read the words of the sculptor Emiliano Luján: "The figure in the monument is an anonymous hero, a warrior who has fallen facedown, gloriously sacrificed in the line of duty, victorious rather than vanquished. . . . In sum, the figure of the martyr fallen at the foot of the national flag." *Patria o muerte*, as Castro would say. Or, as the national anthem of my native country that we chanted as children goes, *We pledge to die with glory*. Smarter ones will come later to sculpt our courage.

*

Why the hell do I think of Michael Jackson in the middle of La Paz, facing the beautiful Church of San Francisco? Where am I? Where are we? Is this the meaning of globalization?

*

I am about to enter San Francisco, one of the oldest churches on the continent. An armed soldier shuts the door in my face. He tells me that it's closing time, that they will open again in the afternoon. Today is Sunday and God has his hours, army willing. At first I feel frustrated. But then I think that this is how literature works: to enter would have been less narrative.

*

In La Paz taxis don't go to where you tell them. You have to negotiate the destination with the drivers. To this plaza, please. "No, not that plaza." To the cathedral, then. "I don't know, I don't know." And the lookout point? Can you take me to the lookout point? "Get in, señor."

*

Here the cars are like cable cars.

*

Public transportation in La Paz is a game of chance. Strictly speaking, there are hardly any city buses, regular lines that take passengers from one stop to another. Things are more complex and more casual. Alongside pedestrians, private vans suddenly appear, full of passengers and headed in every possible direction. From time to time these vans slow down and someone leans out the window to shout, with a booming voice and incredible rapidity, the places the van will go. If you are more or less headed in that direction, for a small fee, you get in. And cross your fingers.

*

I walk down Calle Jaén, which shares its name with the province neighboring Granada, where I live. A name that seems exotic here, but that provokes a smile from this partial Andalusian.

*

When indigenous people bought and sold animals here, the street had a more common name: Kaura Kancha, which in Aymara means "llama market."

*

On the facade of the House of the Green Cross, I read about the street's history: "Tradition has it that in colonial times . . . it was a sinister place because of frequent apparitions and supernatural phenomena (ghosts, goblins, lost souls, infernal noises of horse-led carriages, chains dragging along the ground. But, more than anything, it was known for the presence of a condemned widow who seduced all of the men stumbling out drunk in the wee hours of the night and took them on mysterious adventures. So the residents of the street, inheritors of a strong Catholic faith, decided to put up the green cross to scare off all the malignant creatures that were terrorizing them." That young widow, in a not so ghostly shape, would do something very different from scaring these drunken men. Adultery comes from forces as green as those of this cross.

*

On a plaque in the chimerical Museo del Litoral Boliviano, a poem by Jaime Caballero Tamayo reads, "The sea is further than a night long gone. . . . The sea is closer than tomorrow."

*

Museum of Bolivian Musical Instruments. I stop to look at the *chullu-chullus*, a type of rattle made with the caps of Coca-Cola or Pepsi bottles. This small exhibit is perhaps the only place in Bolivia where indigenous traditions have really devoured multinational companies.

*

I read the description of the *Muyu Muyu charango*: "Two face-to-face or two-faced charangos. One face with diabolical tuning and the other with angelical tuning." A profoundly human instrument. We should all learn to play the Muyu Muyu.

*

I see a miniature of an indigenous person, with a sleepy face and noticeable erection, a glans with an orifice jutting out of his member. It turns out it's an "anthropomorphic whistle."

*

A strongly esoteric message is communicated about indigenous culture. It's a message not only of social, cultural, or anthropological acceptance, but also of sacralization. On the door of the Museum of Ethnography and Folklore is the slogan, "The diverse faces of the soul," together with some indigenous masks. "There used to be doubts about whether the Indian had a soul," says a friend. "Now it's the opposite: the Indian is supposed to have a spirituality that we white people will never have."

*

"The place that scares me the most," she says, "is the hairdresser. The most important women of the neighborhood go to my hairdresser. They are middle class, but they feel upper class. Today one of these women said to the hairdresser, 'Do you know that the Government is going to take our houses away? My daughter sold hers, before that Indian could confiscate it.' And the hairdresser responded, 'They say Evo has a list of all our names and properties. He and the party hate us and are going to take them away. He also says he'll block our bank accounts. Should I do your ends, then?'"

*

The Bolivian "they say" (*dice que*) is similar to the Mexican "it is said" (*dizque*), although it doesn't mean exactly the same thing. Like a lot of sayings here, it has an Aymara origin. In the Aymara language it's improper to say something that one has not seen oneself. For example, you can't say, "Michael Jackson died." You would have to say, "They say that Michael Jackson died." Given the circumstances, that particular news item should have been given only in Aymara.

*

"Michael Jackson, an exploited child?" a friend explodes while reading the paper. "Come on! Have they ever been to La Paz? Have they ever seen the *cholas* with their little kids in the kiosks?" "Once you hit thirty," his wife concludes, "innocence is dangerous."

*

I contemplate the brick constructions attached to the mountain, ascending organically. These orange dwellings expand, snake, and morph as the family gets bigger. First a room. Then a patio. Later a second bedroom. They are genealogical houses, casually remodeled, as mutable as the sky that covers them.

*

In front of the spectacular lookout point El Montículo there is a small church. I stick my head in the entrance. They are in the middle of mass. The priest gives his sermon in a striped sweater. Here, I think, is a priest who is doubly a *moralist*.

*

To blur the line between writing and denunciation can certainly diminish the writer. But also the victims. The mechanical and monographic emphasis on their suffering contributes to petrifying their role, pigeonholing them symbolically. In the novel *El lugar del cuerpo*, by the young Rodrigo Hasbún, the narrator asks himself, "Should he mention the name of his country for the first time? Speak for the first time, through its literature, of the social and economic conditions of his country, awful, unjust, worthy of previous centuries . . . ? Wasn't that what he had always avoided, since his very first book, the appalling tendency of writers from poor countries to do sociology . . . ? For that purpose the simplest notions were better, the fears that all human beings are subject to from the beginning, small phobias and hopes. The need to understand one's own game, which is finally the same for everyone: not what happens in the streets, but in the bedroom, in the bathroom, in the kitchen."

*

In Plaza Abaroa I learn that the man honored, Eduardo Abaroa Hidalgo, hero of the War of the Pacific, died fighting for the

Bolivian sea. Here is the exemplary biography of the Latin American founding father: he was born, he fought, he lost. His defeat shows us the way.

*

Abaroa was not a soldier, but a courageous civilian. An even better reason for him to end up losing. The statue that immortalizes him patiently signals the path to the sea. A story by the La Paz-born writer Marcos Sainz narrates Abaroa's story as if it were a retelling of the tale of the Pied Piper of Hamelin: all Bolivians follow him enthusiastically to the much coveted coast, guided by his clairvoyant finger, and then one by one they drown because they don't know how to swim.

*

We remember the hagiographic fables they miseducated us with in school. I will tell the one about Sergeant Cabral, not really a sergeant but a grenadier, who after saving the life of General San Martín in the midst of battle declared with his dying breath, "I die happy, we have driven away the enemy." I'll mention Martín Kohan's book of short stories, *Muero contento*, which includes a hilarious demy-thologizing of the scene that infuses it with doubt and equivoca-tion. The most interesting thing about (non-)Sergeant Cabral is his genealogy: he was the son of an indigenous Guaraní and an African slave. Both labored under a ranch owner who didn't have to die for the homeland. It is from that ranch owner, and not from the serv-ants who engendered the hero, that the Latin American caudillos descend. A friend tells me that as a girl she adored Abaroa for the celebrated phrase, still taught in the classroom, that he supposedly pronounced before being gunned down by the Chilean troops, "Me, surrender? Let your goddamn grandmother surrender!" As a patriotic quote, I say, it doesn't sound too brilliant. "That's exactly it," my friend responds, "he was the only Bolivian founding father who taught us curse words."

*

Graffiti in the street in the Sopocachi barrio: "There are more radio taxis than feelings." A little later I call a taxi.

*

Graffiti is often more eloquent than opinion pieces. In the area around my hotel I find some graffiti by the feminist collective Mujeres Creando. One example: "After making your dinner / and making your bed / I lost the desire / to make love to you."

*

Another example: "Evo, I need work and dignity, not a voucher of state charity." The state voucher for Bolivian mothers is named after Juana Azurduy, a guerrilla fighter who abandoned her domestic chores to fight in the Wars of Independence. For her role at the front she received the rank of lieutenant colonel, and General Belgrano's sable as well. A third example concludes, "Juana Azurduy was an indomitable beast and not a self-sacrificing mother."

*

In the poet Mónica Velásquez's *Hija de Medea*, I read, "They believed that I was on the rock at the appointed hour / that I surrendered to the ritual of the others and submitted to their mercy. But I, a witch and the daughter of witches, knew. / I divined it early: Father Jason had to be hated . . . "

*

Between the celebration of the bicentennial and the run-up to the electoral campaign, the Bolivian media produces no end of institutional propaganda. I hear a radio commercial in which Evo Morales mentions the exact number of ambulances that the state has acquired over the past year, as if this were a charitable act rather than an investment of citizens' taxes. At the same time, the opposition, as disoriented as it is diminished, denounces the actions of the president as if they were usurpations and not measures taken by the completely legitimate government.

*

"Evo," he says, "has declared war on everyone and has beaten everyone, or at least tried. Army, Church, Santa Cruz, and the cattle ranchers." And how did he win over the military? I ask. "Easy," he responds, "and brilliant: he forced retirement on all senior officers who aspired to be generals and promoted all the junior ones, who are now his most fervent supporters."

*

Southern zone of La Paz. I see convertibles, all-wheel drives, villas, fashion stores, pubs, high-heeled women, buildings like Las Vegas casinos, kids with iPods. And invisible *cholas*. And silent shoe-shiners.

*

This neighborhood in the south is called Insipidville, for the number of stupid people who frequent it. A place populated by adolescents who are more or less happy and alcoholic. Here is where the *jailones* live. *Jailón* comes from the English "high life." But here, alas, I also see more bookstores than in any other part of the city. Alas, anew. Nothing new.

*

Some of the most cosmopolitan and well-read people I know I met in Bolivia and Ecuador. In certain countries culture is almost a luxury item, and those who have it, therefore, are almost princes. One of them, without thinking that he's saying something dreadful, tells me, "Literature flows into us with our mother's milk."

*

At dinner I order llama meat and wine from the Altura vineyards. When traveling without seeing, the menu should be as graphic as possible.

*

Strolling through Sopocachi at night, I come across the Thelonious Jazz Bar. And then La Paz leaves La Paz, and this city could be any city, and we are I don't know where, and that not knowing could (fortunately) also be Latin America.

*

To reach the center of the capital city, the horses in the bicentennial celebrations will have to cover many miles. So many, in fact, that this morning a group of environmentalists are demonstrating in front of the mayor's office. I see them protest on TV, demanding that the horses not be abused. It's a relief to confirm that not even the cause of independence leads to uniform thoughts. When Evo Morales mounted a horse to inaugurate the parades, the opposition asked how an indigenous leader could ride the conquerors' beast.

*

Wilmer Urrelo, National Prize winner for his novel *Ghostly Assassins*, pens an incendiary note today in *La Razón*: "No, I'm not a good resident of La Paz and I don't care. I'd rather say what I think than get excited about a triviality of this proportion. . . . Freedom? Protomartyrdom? Heroes of our revolution? As far as I'm concerned, they can hang Pedro Domingo Murillo again. . . . It's an enormous and absurd waste of money (and worse, of our money) to make such a big deal about the bicentennial. . . . The bicentennial is a government function. Nothing more. Because year 201 will be exactly the same. Murillo will go back to his tomb and we will remember him, even though he did less than Michael Jackson."

*

When I have the afternoon off, in spite of my fatigue, I can't resist the temptation to visit Lake Titicaca. We travel by car to the north. The trip is longer than I anticipated. I unintentionally fall asleep. Suddenly someone touches my shoulder, I open my eyes, and it appears. Imperious, unfathomable, liquid sapphire. The highest navigable lake in the world. They say that Titicaca possesses magnetic, replenishing forces. Many people travel the entire day just to look at it for a little while. The snowy peaks of Huayna defy the general dryness of the land, the yellow and brown, promising a miracle that's all too far away.

*

Along the highway to La Paz, at the edge of El Alto, a statue of Che Guevara grips a machine gun. The figure is made of recycled materials: gears, motor parts, wheels, scraps of metal.

*

The new edition of Plato's *Crito*, the dialogue in which Socrates negates the idea that one should respond to injustices with other injustices, has just been published. The translator is the Bolivian Hellenist and academic Mario Frías Infante. The news gets scarcely a line in the press. That man, I say to myself, is a patriot.

*

The ads on the Bolivian billboards seem to fulfill a therapeutic as well as commercial function. Almost all of the slogans invoke progress, development, and the future. In addition to products, they sell national self-esteem.

*

"From Granada?" asks the driver who takes me to the airport. "My two sisters live there. Imagine that. Over six years now. It was hard at the beginning. Now they're fine. Saving money. I can't go see them because I don't have a visa. One has gotten used to the lifestyle. The other hasn't and wants to come back. I always tell her to stick it out. To stick it out for a little longer."

7

Lima, Club and Copy

WHEN WE LAND amidst the famous fog of Lima, its halogen splendor confirms everything.

*

As usual, I study the immigration forms. I discover a warning that I don't remember having seen in any other country. Spelling mistake included, it says, "In Peru the commercial sexual exploitation of girls, boys, and *adolecents* is a crime penalized by jail time." Just commercial exploitation?

*

"Where are you coming from?" the official asks. From Lima, I answer. The symptoms are getting worse.

*

HOTEL IN LIMA: Casa Andina.
HOTEL ENVIRONMENT: Hazy Good Taste.
RECEPTION STYLE: Sleepy.

*

In the hotel reception, a small sign announces, "Casa Andina works to prevent child sexual abuse." I begin to worry. And then begin to think whether other countries should be the ones worrying.

*

From my bathroom I hear the movements of the bathroom next door with absolute clarity. The wall behind my toilet is closed off with a partition with four round holes, like a hamster cage. I hear someone's tinkling, and someone hears mine.

*

I am staying in the middle of the Miraflores neighborhood, where many of the fiction of Bryce Echenique and Vargas Llosa take place. Right around the corner is Ricardo Palma's house. In this area one feels like one's walking through an anthology of Peruvian literature. And yet one knows that this anthology does exactly the same thing: selects, with extreme partiality, a segment of Peruvian reality.

*

The Peruvian Prime Minister, Yehude Simon, has resigned his post after the conflict in Bagua last month that left thirty-four people dead. "The already-former Prime Minister," informs the EFE, "ensures that over the past nine months he has had 'the opportunity to serve' his country." It appears that nine months can give birth to a life or to the death of thirty-four people. The conflict, I continue reading, took place "between police forces and indigenous people who protested laws allowing the sale of large portions of the rainforest to multinational corporations." Other outlets comment on the appointment of the new prime minister, Javier Velázquez: "Long considered a proponent of dialogue who balanced the public image of the president, he has now become a party man . . . known for his strong-arm tactics at the helm of the Peruvian parliament, as demonstrated by his suspension of seven members of Congress from the Nationalist Party because they protested on the floor of Congress." Protesting in the rainforest would have cost them even more.

*

Discolored, reflexive, indeterminate Lima. Its art is a nuancing of gray.

*

We eat at Pescados Capitales—*Cardinal Fins*—a seafood restaurant. The menu begins with a quote from Joyce: "God made food; the devil the cooks." I scan the selection of sins: Wrath is a tuna prepared à la Karp; Pride, a risotto à la Bonaparte; Lust, fettuccine with Tuna à la Casanova; Envy, a shrimp pot à la Cain; Impatience, a grilled tuna; Greed, a Rockefeller flounder; Sloth, congressional lobster and calamari. As always, I choose impatience.

*

Writers have not appeared in person in this journal. Otherwise, it would have quickly become a chronicle of the trade. But, now that I'm in Lima, how can I not talk about Iván Thays, especially as I scribble these lines in a Moleskine? To a certain degree, Thays's blog, *Moleskine literario*, is the only country inhabited by every Spanish-speaking writer of our generation. I see him come into the restaurant. I rise. We hug. And then, like the protagonist of his novel *Un lugar llamado Oreja de Perro*, he puts on a poker face. And since I know him, I realize it means that we like each other.

*

Un lugar llamado Oreja de Perro is not for people looking for peace and harmony. It's for readers who appreciate the dark pleasure of disquiet. Thays's lyricism is uniquely laconic. His prose comes and goes like a delicate knife. And he manages to transmit a dreamlike unease that simulates the altitude sickness of the protagonist. The novel begins by feigning a political denunciation of a national scope and ends up injecting us with an intimate pain of universal reach. The country lost its people. The character has lost his son. "This," I read, "is the story of one shipwreck inside of another."

*

Waking up in Lima, I discover that my unconscious has also suffered jet lag: I dreamed I was still in La Paz.

*

"Here," someone explains to me, "the upper class continues to be *A World for Julius*. Sunflowers live by looking at the sun. They live by looking toward Miami."

*

I rejoiced in the knowledge that I'm going to the restaurant Rodrigo. There I try, glory be to the kinsmen of the chef and Andean gastric juices, the best octopus I've ever had in my life. It's a grilled baby octopus with kabob sauce. My faith in humanity is restored. Or at least my faith in those who cook.

*

For strictly sociological reasons, I'm going to contradict myself again. Another writer will appear here in person. Specifically, the author of the novel *Lost City Radio*. "In the '94 World Cup," says Daniel Alarcón, the Peruvian novelist who grew up in Alabama, or the American writer who was born in Lima, "I went with my father to see the Colombia-United States match. I was sixteen or seventeen. My father, as you know, is Peruvian. All the Latinos had gone to root for Colombia. It was what we wanted to do, or what we had to do. Root against the Yankees. But suddenly, when the US scored their second goal, I surprised myself by screaming like a crazy person: 'U-S-A! U-S-A!' It was so bad. If you say, '*Viva el Perú, carajo!*' you don't offend anyone, since everyone knows we're losers. But to shout 'U-S-A! U-S-A!' is totally in bad taste. And that's what we all started yelling." I nod, laughing. And then I remember that the first goal of that very match, the US's first goal, was an own goal by the Colombian defender Andrés Escobar. He was gunned down a few days later.

*

In *El Comercio* I read a chronicle of the bicentennial celebrations in La Paz. Correa, the president of Ecuador, declared, "Today the people of Latin America fight together for their second, definitive independence." "As presidents," continued Morales, the host, "we need to succeed with our own armies, doctrines, and policies." *Armies, doctrines, and policies.* The order is worrisome.

*

"Let there be no doubt," Chávez insists, "this coup was carried out by the US Department of State." Honduras as excuse, laboratory, small chessboard for the two great Latin American political blocs. In this game, the Hondurans will be the first pieces taken.

*

The Peruvian media outlets are the only ones on the planet who kept Michael Jackson's death in the background. And they did it, strangely enough, for reasons related to music. The same day that the King of Pop went to sleep forever, the popular folk singer Alicia Delgado was found lifeless in her home. She was also fifty years old, and the circumstances surrounding her death were equally strange. In the case of Alicia Delgado suspicion fell on her supposed lover, the singer Abencia Meza, alias La Pistolita ("The Little Gun"), who now stands accused of ordering the assassination. Globalization has its nuances. So does folk music.

*

In his earlier book of essays, *Mi poncho es un kimono flamenco*, Fernando Iwasaki showed he is the most Japanese Peruvian in Andalusia. In *rePublicanos*, his new book of essays, I read, "When I first settled in Seville, I discovered it was impossible to stop seeing Spain as a Latin American; yet after living here for half of my life, I have discovered, perplexingly, that I also see Latin America as a Spaniard." The book includes a chronological classification of Latin American literature. The last generation is described thus: "Novelists born after the sixties who understand literature as a stateless, eccentric, and extraterritorial creation." Iwasaki's name should be in bold.

*

In Lima, as in La Paz, the most common form of public transportation is the unpredictable van with a human loudspeaker. The traffic is equally chaotic. Peru seems similar to Bolivia, but with a middle class. This year the Peruvian economy will grow, along with the Bolivian, in the midst of a global recession. This statistic lends itself to naive or demagogic interpretations. Bowing down a little and trying to lift one's head from the ground are not the same thing.

*

News arrives about the common grave where, in theory, the remains of Federico García Lorca lie. For a moment, I feel like I'm back in Granada. Beyond the love for Lorca's poetry, which is ubiquitous in Latin America, I'm surprised by the interest in the court case. "Here," someone explains, "we also have our war dead and our hidden graves."

*

It drizzles. And it drizzles. "If we at least had clear, decisive rain," my friend complains, "it wouldn't be such a bitch. But this constant feeling of being stung in the face, what bullshit, my God!"

*

This July 28 is the 188th anniversary of Peru's independence. Without a doubt, July is the month of the independences of the Americas. The traditional independence-day parade is supposed to take place on the twenty-ninth, led by a group of obsolete tanks, the mission of which is to defend national security, or exactly the opposite. But today, it was decided that the parade had to be postponed because of the imminent deployment of swine flu. If the flu defeats the tanks, I will have had a pacifist idea.

*

Flu, independence. Independence, flu.

*

Am I fleeing the flu or following its trail?

*

"Here everybody licks Mario Vargas Llosa's ass," I am told. It would be interesting to ask why, then, they didn't vote for him when he ran for president. A question that President Fujimori must have asked himself every day with a hideous laugh.

*

I wander down to Redondo and Agua Dulce beaches. I run toward the sea, the deserted sea. In the winter, beaches have something moving and open about them. They remind us of a posthumous life, the world without us. I step onto the dark sand. I look out at the freezing water of the Pacific. It's an ocean I barely know, with which I've never conversed. How can we live without the sea? That's what we ask ourselves every time we look at it. On the other side of the horizon, on the island of El Frontón, the Shining Path terrorists were massacred in a prison as remote and present as this mist.

*

A surfer slips into the cold waves. I think I'm starting to see things, but someone explains that surfers come to these beaches in the winter. I look again. I no longer see him.

*

I look at the footprints of my shoes in the hard sand, sculpted by the water. They won't last long: they're mine.

*

The Peruvian master José Watanabe, who died a few years back, left behind some unpublished poems. One of them said, "Not chosen to be contemplated, / seen / without ideas, the stones / would never be remembered by that man. When he left, / the three remained immaculate upon the sand."

*

A friend has problems with domestic workers. Here, as in many Latin American countries, they continue to live in the house of their employers from Monday to Saturday. For six days a week, their personal life is voided, absorbed by the incessant and promiscuous work relationship. A form of slavery, we might say, with vacations. During my infancy in Argentina, I myself was raised by maids. Just remembering makes me uneasy. "Sometimes you wish they didn't have a life, you know," my friend says. "When they begin to do their own thing, they start causing problems."

*

As a form of patriotic homage, a poster as big as it is startling hangs in the Kennedy park: "Nobody who is against Peru is right." The quote is from Andrés Avelino Cáceres, a caudillo in the war against Chile.

*

In Rafael Robles Olivos's *Aquí murió el payaso*, published by the indispensable publishing house Estruendomudo, I read a prayer for those fallen in combat: "My son / who art on the ground, / forgive us of our guilt / our crimes. / Obey your mother / and jump the abyss . . . / Today was simply / a good day / to kill."

*

I find out that, by law, every building must fly a Peruvian flag or else pay a fine. The Spanish often praise the affinity that Latin Americans feel for the flags of their home countries, unlike Spaniards themselves. Maybe it's not a bad idea to treat the national colors cautiously. Where flags are concerned, it's easy to go from pride to decree.

*

I visit the last house of Ricardo Palma, narrator of the memorable Peruvian traditions I once studied. In the interior patio rises a *floripondio*, a big tall flower, possibly planted by the author himself (yes, according to the guard; no, according to the guide), and to which an absurd legend attributes his daughters' failure to marry. I review Palma's biography. He lived a Borgesian life with his family in the National Library, where he was the director. His compatriots sent him into exile in Chile for his liberal sympathies. Later, during the War of the Pacific, the Chileans sacked his library and burned his old home down. Art has no homeland. Which is why any homeland can fuck an artist up.

*

I nose around in Palma's library. I see two volumes of the 1895 edition of the dictionary of the Real Academia Española, of which Palma was a member. I see Diderot's entire encyclopedia, published in Paris in

1875. And Voltaire's complete works in French. On top of the desk there is a facsimile edition of *Don Quixote*: Barcelona, 1608. I also find some books that surprise me for their modernity, or perhaps for their bad taste: H.G. Wells's *The Island of Doctor Moreau*, a novel by Fernán Caballero, the poems of Campoamor. There are several works by Poe, and of course, a lot of History. But the author most represented seems to be Ricardo Palma himself.

*

Palma's daughter, Angélica, was also a novelist, a political analyst, and one of the most brilliant journalists in the country. Among the museum's papers, there is a poem that José Zorrilla dedicated to Angélica. Vain as always, the old man wrote in his own hand, "In your Country, the land of sun, / your father told you of me / and to see me you desired, / to come here with him." Don Zorrilla couldn't help commemorating himself, even when he tried to pay homage to someone else.

*

When the poet José Gálvez married, his friend Palma gave him the pen with which he had written his texts. A wonderful note accompanied it, which ended, "I foresee that my pen, when wielded by José Gálvez, will always honor the memory of my name."

*

2666 on the front table at a bookstore in Lima. I pick up a copy, feel its consistency, and think about death. I remember a theater version of the novel by Àlex Rigola, as incredible as it was excessive, and therefore faithful to the work itself. I reread the inside cover.

Then I see the price: 207 soles. Sixty-nine dollars. The tragedy of importation. At that price, not a single young Bolaño fan could ever buy the novel. They will see it as a distant star.

*

Passing by Juan Ramón Ribeyro's *Prosas apátridas*, I can't resist the temptation to open it for a moment. It's something I do frequently with this magisterial book, as if it were the *I Ching*. I read a passage about the overwhelming proliferation of publications: "My own library . . . is becoming infested with parasitic books, which arrive here who knows how and contribute, through a phenomenon of attraction and agglutination, to cementing the mountain of illegibility and, among these books, the lost books, I find the ones I've written. . . . To enter a bookshop is frightening and paralyzing for any writer, it's like being on the threshold of oblivion."

*

In *A World For Julius*, when the grandfather's mansion is demolished, the family moves to the Country Club, which has now been converted into a hotel. I go to dinner at the hotel with a wide-eared smile of happiness, as Bryce Echenique himself might say. It faces the golf club, whose boring vistas the Lima upper class will still do anything to possess. Lima is a club of clubs.

*

During the nineties, while terrorism, the Dirty War, and the economic crisis devastated the country that the former current president Alan García had fled, the Country Club was abandoned. The facade was falling apart. It was even rumored that it would be demolished. An international consortium rescued the building and refurbished part of it to open this hotel. Today wealthy tourists and businessmen pay three hundred dollars a night. And they don't even get the luxury of thinking about Bryce Echenique.

*

I watch Josué Méndez's first film, *Días de Santiago*, a version of *Taxi Driver*, Lima-style. It tells of the tragedy of a former soldier who, after years of combating terrorists, feels incapable of reintegrating into civilian life. When he's in his taxi, he never repeats the same itinerary. "Isn't it longer this way?" a young woman asks him. "I always take a different route," he explains, "and there's nothing wrong with that. It makes me feel more comfortable. That's all. And if someone tells me not to, that nobody is following me, I tell that person they're crazy, why not, come on. There's always someone out there. Always someone behind you."

*

In the studio of the radio station RPP, I run into a pro-Fujimori congressman named Carlos Raffo, who defends his boss with sinister eloquence. The congressman admits that former president Fujimori paid fifteen million dollars to his former adviser Vladimiro Montesino. An individual who, to be fair, had an incredibly appropriate name for someone working in intelligence services. After acknowledging the illegal payments, the congressman adds, "It's been legally proven that Fujimori is guilty. But now we must find out of what."

*

In the best (read: most expensive) zone of Barranco, I stop to observe the three-story house of Don Mario. A magnificent, though not ostentatious, building designed by his cousin Freddy Cooper. Notwithstanding political differences, he deserves it, and a Scottish castle to boot. Two large cacti, perhaps metaphorical, guard the living quarters. The side that faces the ocean, where Vargas Llosa looks when he writes, sits on the Mario Vargas Llosa Esplanade. When the writer turned seventy, the mayor decided to pay homage to him by renaming the esplanade. After the elections, the next mayor restored the old name; his view was that you had to be dead to get your own street. A requirement that Vargas Llosa wasn't willing to meet. This stupid municipal decision created a controversy. In the end, it was agreed that the esplanade would be called Mario Vargas Llosa for a few blocks (around the writer's house) and the rest would keep the name Paul Harris. Being posthumous while living isn't easy. Nor is being Peruvian.

*

El Virrey is a happy mix of Peruvian and Uruguayan bibliophiles. In Montevideo there are other branches of this family bookstore, one of which I had the pleasure of visiting. And now here, in El Virrey on Calle Dasso, among its restorative shelves, I go crazy, crazy, crazy. I lose all sense of my luggage's capacity. And I begin to buy everything I haven't bought before. New books, used books. Peruvian literature and world literature. Spanish books that are no longer sold in Spain. And first editions. With fear-tinged excitement, I pick up the original edition of Vallejo's *The Black Heralds*. I open it at the beginning and read a quote from the Gospel: "*Qui potest capere capiat.*" Let him who can comprehend

comprehend. Even though Vallejo's miracle will always be incomprehensible.

*

I caress an original copy of *Trilce*. I read on the inside cover, "Typographical Printers of the Penitentiary. Lima. 1922." I'm simply unable to keep reading.

*

Blue Quickies? I ask my friend. That sounds like a Smurf orgy. What the hell are blue quickies? My friend shrugs his shoulders and takes me. He takes me to the Blue Quickie market. Which is . . . what? My friend defines it as an "informall." They sell everything, *every thing*. But it's all fake. A pirated replica of the world. A clandestine version of capitalism. I browse among the hundreds of stands. I go to a music stand. A young kid compares prices, turns around, and asks why one CD is more expensive than the others. "Ah," says the employee, "that's because it's an original copy."

*

There is no movie in the history of film, including small Latin American productions, that can't be found in the Blue Quickies. My friend and I look at each other, euphoric and stunned, anxious and furtive. That's it. We've crossed the line. I am, we are, pirates. I'm not ashamed. And of that I'm ashamed.

*

Later in the night I watch Claudia Llosa's first film, *Madeinusa*, which I like even more than *The Milk of Sorrow*. The story takes place in a fictional indigenous village. Everything occurs over the Sacred Time, a weekend of impunity during which all of the inhabitants shut their eyes to Christ because, as the protagonist explains, "he no longer sees us. God is dead. Until Sunday." Pure Nietzsche in the Andes. A well-dressed Limeñan comes to the village. His name is Salvador, he's blond, and he doesn't seem willing to save anyone. While Christ's eyes are closed, Salvador takes Madeinusa's virginity, anticipating her own father, who will abuse his daughter that same night. The film is an anthropological melodrama. A risky parable about superstitions, including the superstition of the guilty outsider. "The foreigner has killed my father," the protagonist and her sister unanimously lie. Madeinusa is a Malinche who doubly avenges herself, against the internal and external patriarchy, using both of them as they've used her. Then she flees to Lima on a bus, possibly with a child in her womb. The main actress just released an album of Quechua music. One of the songs is called "The Wind that Blows."

*

"This is not the script of my life," I read in Gustavo Rodríguez's novel *Your Mother's Laughter*. "This script *is* my life."

*

At this point, my routine with drivers who take me to the airport is almost spouse-like. They begin by making guarded observations about the weather. Then they become interested in my impression of the city. And finally they ask me questions about what it's like to be a writer. I try to avoid the topic, or at least shorten it, and get them to talk about politics. On this occasion, the Lima driver's diagnosis is the following: "The first Fujimori administration was very good. He fought against the inflation and terrorism that were destroying us. The bad thing was that he later tried to *perpetrate himself* in power."

*

Lima airport. The newsstand. To travel the world today is to witness the same debates in different languages and dialects. In the newspaper *Perú 21* I read an article about piracy, a hot topic at the moment. The author begins by criticizing the digital canon statutes and concludes by stating, "Everybody can now take ownership of culture, transform it, produce original works, and share them with the world so that someone else can take ownership and repeat the cycle." It is undoubtedly questionable to charge extra for a private copy (or for a *possible* private copy, as some countries have started doing in the expectation of piracy). But to argue that digital technology allows anyone not only to possess but also to remake a work of art seems to me an uncritical commonplace. Would we Internet users be fine if *anyone* came into the kitchen of a restaurant and *freely* finished preparing our meal? Or *completed* the electric installation in their house? Or *transformed* court sentences? Or operated on their liver and *modified* the diagnosis? For all of that there are artisans, specialists. But, oh, culture is different. Painting, music, and literature are things anyone can do. They aren't as serious as science, law, electricity, gastronomy.

*

While in Spain, like every other year, thousands of hectares of green land (are there still thousands?) catch fire; in the south and central regions of Peru, the fear is floods that could be caused by the onslaught of El Niño. Between these two opposite and similar phenomena, victim and victimizer, humanity is gearing up for the third catastrophe.

*

In the boarding area I read *Elogios criminales*, a collection of chronicles by Julio Villanueva Chang, who claims (or recommends) to live in Lima as if he were permanently visiting. The book ends with a judicious warning: "Being curious is not an occupation that you can declare to an immigration agent." Neither is being a chronicler.

8

Quito, Volcanoes, and Dividers

A SMALL NOVELTY in Ecuador's immigration forms. In a printout provided by Avianca Airlines, for the first time I find a box specifically addressed to women. A box that reminds me of my childhood in Argentina and the lives of my grandmothers:

MR/MRS/MS

FIRST AND LAST NAME

_____

MAIDEN NAME

_____

*

I've already been to Quito and I realize that, at the beginning, this prevents me from seeing it. I'll pretend I've never been here. Maybe that's what traveling is: pretending we've never seen anything before.

*

The first time I flew into Quito, I remember my surprise at the dense fog wrapped around the peaks of Pichincha Volcano. I had formed a stereotyped image of the Ecuadorian capital as being sunnier, more tropical. But today it is sunny, with the same sun I expected to find on my first trip here.

*

When I arrive at the hotel, they offer me tomato juice. A delicacy that is not exactly sweet, just like this city.

*

HOTEL IN QUITO: Swissôtel.
HOTEL ENVIRONMENT: Elevated, in Every Sense.
RECEPTION STYLE: Fruity.

*

Do you have chocolate cake? I ask the waiter. "No," he answers, "but we have figs and cheese."

*

Street vendors have been expelled from the downtown area (here they prefer to say "relocated") and moved to another, less visible area (here they prefer to say "their own space"). The mayor who made this decision also pushed through the remodeling of the historic district, one of the most beautiful and brightly lit in the continent. The mayor belongs to the Democratic Left party. Before that he was a general, and gained notoriety during the border conflict with Peru. Obviously, he's an expert in displacing his enemies.

*

I walk through the presidential palace during the changing of the guard. I hear a blast of trumpets and think of Holy Week in Spain. The military and the Church are off-key in similar ways.

*

Seen from above in the dead of night, the south of Quito burns candles to its destiny.

*

On Panecillo Hill I have a religious vision in pop guise: the Virgin of Quito. Metallic. Winged. Huge. Stomping a half-moon with her not quite feather-light legs. Vanquishing with a chain the serpent of evil, who writhes, retreats, and shrinks. With a crown of twelve stars twirling around her head. As if Mary had been smoking a bit of Mary Jane.

*

Next to the flying virgin the neon lights of the bicentennial glimmer: "August 10, 1809. Quito Revolution." It's hard not to have respect and admiration when people talk about the independence movement. But when twelve balls of identical flames are doing the talking, one begins to develop a healthy dose of counterrevolutionary skepticism.

*

From El Panecillo, the historic center suggests its own castling of light. The amazing city grid attempts to dominate the downtown slopes. The Spaniards called this "playing chess with Quito."

*

Here light floods the early morning. Breakfast begins at five (five!). Ecuador is a country that gets up early, yet continues to postpone its awakening.

*

In some countries, it's not appropriate to say no. Nobody ever says no in Bolivia, Peru, or Ecuador, though they also don't say yes. Some people attribute it to extreme courtesy. I would call it a habit of oppression.

*

"Quito is like La Paz, only green," a Bolivian friend summarized. There's some truth to that. This city does evoke a more peaceful La Paz. Although only in appearance: Quito is surrounded by active volcanoes. Seven years ago, Pichincha began to cough, a voluminous plume arose, and for weeks there was ash everywhere.

*

Someone gives me *Historias bajo el árbol*, an anthology that brings together short-story writers from Ecuador and Peru under the auspices of each country's consulate. A positive venture for two neighbors that maintained an interminable border dispute for over a century and a half. The book was published last year, exactly a decade after the definitive peace treaty. Literature is always in conflict, always on the border, and always at odds with its neighbors. But it has yet to kill anyone.

*

I read the Ecuadorian authors of *Historias bajo el árbol*. In Eduardo Varas's story, "the avenue is a dragon. It spits fire," and one of the characters "walks at midday, in the midst of the waking dragon." I wouldn't pay much attention to this if Solange Rodríguez Pappe's story didn't end with a pregnant woman who announces while touching her belly, "It's a dragon like its father." I confirm that the same novelist published a book titled *Dracofilia*. This coincidence also wouldn't have meant much to me if I hadn't found these lines in a poetry volume by Aleyda Quevedo Rojas: "I still hear / the sharp dragons / boring into my entrails." And then, another book of poetry by Dina Bellrham: "I, tired of killing dragons." The idea reappears in the various books I read throughout the day. It occurs to me that Ecuadorian literature is a literature of dragons. That it has waited for years, decades, centuries, holding its breath. A breath fiery with waiting. Capable of setting fire to anything. Tired of remaining contained within itself. A literature turned volcano.

*

In the foothills of the volcano, on the celebrated Cima de la Libertad, a monument commemorates the Battle of Pichincha, when Ecuador gained its freedom from the Spanish yoke. It's in the middle of the barrio La Libertad. I ask what the barrio is like. The answer is cautious: "Cheap." That is, poor, miserable. I didn't expect anything less from a patriotic symbol.

*

Gabriela Alemán's novel *Poso Wells* poses an eruptive question. What happens to a city when its hidden monsters abruptly emerge? The text on the back cover completes the metaphor: "Everything here is as jumbled and incandescent as the volcanic lava to which the story leads us." There are realities that burn. Maybe that's why in the beginning of the book a politician bursts into flames during a campaign stunt in Poso Wells, leaving behind a lingering smell of burnt flesh. What kind of place is Poso Wells? Where is it? It could be a nightmarish version of Guayaquil. Or Guayaquil's nightmare. Or the prolongation of H.G. Wells's Andean fantasies. Whatever the case, the place "doesn't appear on any map." But nevertheless, "it is there, contrary to many people's desires . . . in the most foul and forgotten hole that exists this side of the Central Pacific." I return to a story by Miguel Antonio Chávez, the author of the aforementioned anthology, in which the protagonist receives an invitation to a certain American university. The purpose is to bring together writers from countries whose literature "has little to no circulation on the continent." The program includes representatives from five countries: Belize, Guyana, Suriname, Bolivia, and Ecuador. To add insult to injury, the conference was organized because of a "surplus in the university's funds, which would have gone to another school if not used this year." Unlike the Argentine, Colombian, Mexican, and Spanish writers, young Ecuadorian writers aren't looking for fame. They just want to exist.

*

I ask if the country is better off than it was a few years ago. The answer is yes and no. I ask, more specifically, if aside from the progress of the well-to-do, the number of poor people has gone up or down. The answer is that first it went up, then it went down, and now it's stable. I ask if Correa's policies have influenced these fluctuations. "Our presidents," they answer, "limit themselves to administering oil revenues. And last year the price of oil went through the roof."

*

To cross the street in Quito, or pretty much any Latin American capital, is to feel a bit like a citizen of the country. One advances by risking one's life, and absolutely no rules apply.

*

In Rafael Lugo's novel *Veinte*, I read, "A little while ago I ran over three men with my car. It happened in the course of an honest day's work."

*

An editorial in the newspaper *Hoy* affirms, "The authorities of Guayaquil are looking to extend services and well-being to sectors of the population other than those inhabitants who already enjoy them because of the city's robust and renowned infrastructure. . . . However, this requires not only decision making, but also the support of the whole community, so that no decision not made by the city will impede, let alone block, the irrepressible development of the 'Pearl of the Pacific', the most dynamic and populous city of Ecuador, whose management policies . . . " Such elocution about Guayaquil is not innocent. The mayor of Guayaquil, Jaime Nebot, is President Correa's greatest rival.

*

I recall my impressions of Guayaquil from a visit last year. The city is controlled by two impulses, which coexist with a controlled but perceptible tension: the recent movement toward prosperity and the ever-present reality of poverty. A poverty of begging children, single mothers, and juvenile delinquency. Mayor Nebot's strategy seems similar to that of other emerging places: to erect a happy and vigilant fence within whose limits the "dynamic population" moves. That way foreign tourists can visit the fabulous boardwalk around the Guayas River without fear. This is the modern Guayaquil being promoted. One that, without being false, also isn't true.

*

I read *Quadrilátero*, a collection of Ecuadorian essays. I pause on a text by Cristóbal Zapata, who is also a poet and novelist. Fascinated by the strange case of Héctor Bianciotti, who first left his country and then left his language, Zapata writes, "The disinterest and even disdain for Bianciotti's work probably obeys certain unspoken ideological codes. On the one hand, his tacit disagreement with Peronism—one of the Argentine national religions—but even more importantly his adoption of French as a literary language. Perhaps in his native country, they don't forgive this double desertion." One of Ecuador's cultural virtues is its gift of foreignness, its sensitivity toward immigrants, fugitives, and stateless individuals. The cosmopolitanism of its writers is a form of survival more than of prestige. As if all of Ecuador's literature, in the brilliant periphery of our language, dreamed of writing in a different language. Or of moving the center.

*

I come upon the work of a bizarre bilingual poet I have never heard of, let alone read: Alfredo Gangotena. He was born in

Quito in 1904. He traveled to Paris as an adolescent. He stayed there for seven years. Then he returned to his native city, where he died at the age of forty. He had a hybrid aesthetic profile: avant-garde and Catholic, surrealist and mystical. After leaving Ecuador, Gangotena turned to French, a language he would write in much more frequently than his mother tongue. I read *Crueldades*, a volume of Spanish translations of several of Gangotena's previously unknown poems. The book begins with a splendid rhyme impossible to reproduce: "J'apprends la grammaire / de ma pensée solitaire." Grammar and solitude rhyme? To be translated into one's mother tongue. Maybe that's what happens to a poet every time he's read.

*

Here, as in Bolivia, Argentina, and Venezuela, almost all of the media outlets belong to the opposition. Except for *El Telégrafo*, every paper sports a headline that signals confrontation with the government. "I wish," says a friend, "information was more balanced in Ecuador." "Balance doesn't exist," responds another. "Neither does information," a third concludes.

*

I share airtime on TV with the editor of the magazine *Vanguardia*. He ceaselessly attacks Correa and his supporters, whom he accuses of violating free speech. His tone irritates me. I find him agitated in his gestures, aggressive in his arguments. A few hours later, coincidentally, I meet a journalist from *Vanguardia*. In the car, she tells me that a few weeks before armed men erupted into the paper's editorial office. Startled, I ask her if they hurt anyone. "Luckily, no," she responds. "They just took computers, files, and documents." The light turns red and she suddenly hits the brakes.

*

I attend a dinner at the Jacarandá private development. We stop the car by the guard post. We give our names. We are questioned. We cross a barrier. Finally, we enter the development. This is what they call comfortable living.

*

In my room I discover, amid magazines and the Bible, a copy of *César Dávila Andrade, combate poético y suicidio*. The author is Jorge Dávila Vázquez, and the book comprises the life and work of the great Ecuadorian poet. I'm surprised to find a book like this in the hotel. Does the company have an interest in poetry? The answer is in the handwritten dedication: "To Gonzalo, united in a shared love for the word and its combats. With affection," and then the essayist's own signature. In Chapter Two, I read the epigraph, "Personality of the strange writer in a provincial, bourgeois, and conventional environment. Contacts, affinities, and rejections." At least in terms of rejection, it seems like this Gonzalo continued the tradition.

*

I listen as the deposed Zelaya, who continues to plan his return to Honduras, forgets the end of the Lord's Prayer in front of the press. Considering all that's coming to him, he'll need to know it very well.

*

A video was just released in which Mono Jojoy, the leader of the FARC in Colombia, mentions economic backing his organization supposedly provided for Correa's electoral campaign. The *Wall Street Journal* had already referred to the purported support that Ecuador's government had provided to the FARC, apparently helping them take refuge along the border with Colombia and end the fumigation of the coca crop, the main financial source of the guerrilla organization. The president has assured he will bring a suit against the US newspaper for disseminating such slander, whose objective is to "destabilize the progressive Latin American governments." The suit has not yet been filed. The appearance of the video also isn't a coincidence. The Colombian police seized it while Ecuador was attempting to prosecute the former Colombian minister of defense. Latin America is a detective novel. Only, rather than outsiders, its protagonists are those in power.

*

Ring. Ring. Ring. Yes? I say into the phone, speaking from the recesses of my soul. "Good day, señor: your wake-up call." After so much early rising, Quito ends up waking up inside of you.

*

In the Quito airport there are checkpoints that prevent you from entering the ticket-counter area. Nobody is allowed to accompany passengers while they wait to check their bags. Over the past few years emigration rose to such a degree that scores of relatives, lovers, and friends used to circle around the airline counters. Not satisfied with this degree of separation, airport officials installed a series of high dividers, which now prevent passengers and those who have come to say goodbye from seeing one another. Before there was too much crying, too much drama. There still is. But now there is a divider, a barrier. This is progress.

*

I read a poem by Augusto Rodríguez titled "Aeropuerto de Barajas": "They were called one by one / they were searched from their feet to their souls / they were abused physically and psychologically / the last I heard they would be returned / like lost packages, to their place of origin / to their imaginary Ecuador / to their beloved and distant Ecuador / which surely doesn't expect them."

9

Caracas, the Horse before the Mirror

AT THE AVIANCA TICKET COUNTER, when I request my boarding passes for the flight to Caracas, I learn that it's mandatory to show a return ticket. Otherwise, you're not allowed to board. You must prove that you'll leave Venezuela before you even arrive. When such things happen in the United States or Europe, we consider them humiliating, imperialist, fascist. Opposite poles feed off of each other, copy each other, admire each other in secret. *Gracias*, Hugo. Here's my ticket. *Puedo entrar?*

*

Passenger admitted. Boarding area. Newsstand. Headline from today, July 22, in Guayaquil's *El Universal:* "A Spanish Immigrant Auctions off her Virginity." According to the article, she's doing it to help her mother.

*

Meanwhile, from Spain, the cover of *El Mundo:* "A Shameful Photo." "Moratinos," the minister of foreign affairs, "ends three centuries of anticolonialist fervor by posing with a smile on the Rock," that is, Gibraltar. I don't recall the word "shameful" being used in any of the paper's headlines when Aznar was photographed with Bush and Blair in the Azores before invading Iraq.

*

I turn my head and see *ABC*: "The Government Squanders 300 Years of Fighting for Gibraltar in One Day." "Moratinos," they add, "puts cooperation before Spain's historical claims to the Rock." Two problems here. First, if it's really been three centuries, then the "struggle" hasn't really been producing results, right? Maybe it's time for a change in strategy. Second, why do some people pronounce the word "cooperation" as if they were saying "disgrace" or "bombing"? Mysteries of the press.

*

While waiting to board, I observe the other people in line. In this part of Latin America pretty much every breast and behind looks like it's been inflated with helium. Curves that never descend. Monstrous protuberances. The mother of a cute black-eyed young girl has a tattoo of the Star of David on her ankle. Behind her, a priest shields a volume of William Blake under his armpit.

*

As is typical in this age of flu, they hand us a health form. I examine it in surprise. Less than a full page and badly copied, it's almost impossible to read and the information seems incomplete. Without a doubt it's the worst form I've filled out up to this point. The Venezuelan government, with all its oil and taxes, has enough money to do better in the face of an epidemic. At the top of the form it states, "Bolivarian Government of Venezuela. Ministry of Popular Power for Health and Social Protection." Of course they couldn't just call it the Ministry of Health.

*

I read in the Venezuelan customs form, "Specify here any new articles that you and your family are carrying in your luggage." One assumes, one would like to assume, that they're trying to prevent illegal trade. That's why you must declare *new* items. But the English translation offered is the following: "*Any* article that you and your family members are bringing into the country." Anything, everything. Foreign tourists, at least English-speaking ones, must therefore describe the entire contents of their suitcases. Which, among other categories, includes: 5. Books, magazines, and documents in general. (I can't understand why it's necessary for national security purposes to declare what we're reading.) 8. Musical instruments. 11. Portable Typewriters. (Typewriters? Why not record players? Kinetoscopes?) 12. Articles for individual sports. In light of this questionnaire, entering the country is beginning to seem like a sport. And a high-risk one.

*

Above the immigration line at the Caracas airport, a sixty-foot-high poster shows Hugo Chávez pointing to the horizon with his index finger. "Venezuela became free, free forever!" the motto proclaims. It's not without its logic. This explains perpetual re-election.

*

I adjust my watch to Chávez's time zone: half an hour later than in Bogotá, half an hour earlier than in La Paz. An exquisite touch. Time to leave this airport.

*

On the way to the hotel. Midnight. "I'm going faster," the driver explains, "so they don't try anything." I had turned on the inside lights. He turned them off. A portion of the highway looks wet, though it's not raining. "They wet it," the driver observes, "to cause accidents." Who are "they"? I ask. "They, they," he repeats, as if in a trance, "the poor people."

*

Despite its impeccable appearance, as soon as I set foot in the hotel I feel something strange. I'm not sure what. Something. A certain sense of displacement. As if tomorrow morning the entire edifice were going to be destroyed. As if the employees knew some terrible fact they were forced to keep from me. I don't give this feeling too much thought, and attribute it to the untimely hour of my arrival. But there's something here. I don't know what. Something.

*

HOTEL IN CARACAS: Caracas Palace.
HOTEL ENVIRONMENT: Oil-rich Stanley Kubrick.
RECEPTION STYLE: Phantasmagoric.

*

Since the indefensible coup attempt against Chávez, there have been two different dollars in Venezuela. The international one, which all of us mortals know. And the imaginary one, regulated by the National Currency Commission. The international dollar is worth seven bolívares in the black market. The imaginary dollar, officially labeled "preferred," is just above two bolívares. This was the way local currency was revalued internally. But in the rest of the world, its devaluation continues. If one wishes to exchange dollars or pay in foreign currency, the conversion is done according to the imaginary rate. Then our bills are exchanged on the black market, instantly tripling their value. Marxists call this "surplus value."

*

I ask a friend what he does to find out the real value of the bolívar, given that its value is trapped between the black market and the state mirage. "Easy, my friend," he responds, "I look at how much a McDonald's hamburger costs. Whatever the hamburger costs, that's what the bolívar is really worth in dollars. Now, for example, it's just over four bolívares."

*

"When God created Venezuela," someone says, "he was totally high."

*

I'm told about the incredible story of Esdras Parra. She was born a man, and as a man she achieved great fame as a short-story writer. During that period she became a staple of mainstream Venezuelan culture. Later she began to take hormones. Finally she submitted (or perhaps the opposite) to a sex-change operation, hoping to win the acceptance of the lesbian woman with whom she had fallen in love. Like in Tod Browning's moving film *The Unknown*, Parra suffered the rejection of the woman whose love had motivated her to undergo surgery. Not only was she dismissed by the object of her affection, but also by her former peers. But she kept going, secure in her new identity. She learned to speak again, modulating her voice like a woman. Then she stopped writing short stories forever, writing only poetry until the day she died. I listen with wide eyes and gaping mouth. When I get back to the hotel I look up her poems. I write down these three lines: "There is comfort in your language / it willingly abides by / its own rigor." On the blog *Ciudad Escrita* I read an article by Carlos Flores, originally published by the magazine *Exceso*: "Esdras Parra had such balls that when she decided to get rid of them, she did."

*

In Bolivia almost all intellectuals support Evo Morales, with certain reservations. In Argentina they're divided between the government and the opposition. In Ecuador, they ignore Correa with a certain disdain. In Venezuela, they resist Chávez with a dose of humor.

*

Various publishers and editors tell me that importing books is tricky in Venezuela. Taxes, laws, and customs all conspire to limit importation. Mysterious customs regulations hold books up for weeks—if, that is, they actually arrive. This means that distributors often end up looking for copies on the black market. They buy them at top American dollar, making them more expensive for the reading public. The idea is that such restrictions, even beyond maintaining ideological control, favor domestic publishing houses. But domestic houses often either can't undertake large publishing ventures or spend years in the process, because they have incredible difficulties importing paper. We must recognize that, as a circular tale, this literary politics is amazing.

*

The government has its own printing house. They print books for the Librerías del Sur network, where the entire inventory is cheap, almost free. This state program serves to popularize reading. And it would be completely admirable, if it didn't also entail an unfair advantage over the rest of the publishing houses and a squeeze on all other bookstores, whose survival is constantly in doubt. It's as troubling that there are readers who can't afford books as it is that the publishing funds are determined by the president. Luckily Chávez claims to be a great reader. In fact, he recently stated that he had read *Les Misérables* (which is about a thousand pages long) before going to bed.

*

"The worst part," says a friend, "is that we can't even support the opposition. We aren't *chavistas*, but here the opposition groups are total fascists."

*

In the municipality of Chacao, a ritzy neighborhood, we are afforded the luxury of having breakfast out in the open. This is not a metaphor. They say, "The luxury of having a nice breakfast out in the open." We sit at one of the outside tables. I instinctively look up, as if expecting bombs. An ironic pigeon defecates on my shoulder.

*

"We call this zone—Altamira, Chacao, and its environs—the Other City," they explain. I deduce that They don't live here.

*

I browse some of the country's novels. *En la casa del pez que escupe el agua*, a historical novel by the deceased writer Francisco Herrera Luque, grabs my attention. I read the beginning and a character named Andrés appears. This doesn't happen too often, so I continue. The novel narrates the birth of oil-rich Venezuela and the political process that brought Juan Vicente Gómez to power. This same dictator, who governed Venezuela for a third of a century, inspired García Márquez's *Autumn of the Patriarch*. Gómez died in power at an extremely old age, between November and the beginning of December 1935. The exact day is a mystery, because the general ordered in his will that the date of his death must coincide with Bolívar's: December 17. It's often said in jest that General Gómez is the only Venezuelan president who governed after his death. Until now.

*

Whoever you are, whatever you do, and however you see things, in Venezuela you cannot *not* talk about Chávez. That is perhaps his main victory and his greatest act of oppression.

*

"Public hospitals here," a friend tells me, "are falling apart. They have nothing. But the government donates ambulances to Bolivia." Are these the same ambulances that Evo Morales announced over the radio as the great Bolivian investment in health services?

*

Tomorrow is a national holiday commemorating the birth of the liberator of liberators, Simón Bolívar. It seems that I'm collecting viruses and patriotisms over the course of my journey. If in fact they are two different things.

*

From my room I can just make out Monte Ávila, which I knew first as a publishing house before I realized it was a mountain. Its nervous greenness surprises me. I suddenly recall a Venezuelan joke about the Argentine ego. Why do Argentineans climb to the top of El Ávila? To see how the city looks without them.

*

One of the stories in Rodrigo Blanco's *Los invencibles* tells of a mountaineer who gets lost on El Ávila. When they finally rescue him, it's too late: the character has literally lost himself; that is, he has lost a part of his identity. The story ends with an insane act that is in reality an indication of sanity: the mountaineer decides to join the rescue crews with the secret hope "of finding myself again and being able, once and for all, to go back." The story can be read as a high-altitude variation on the theme of the double. But it's also a parable of the alienation of the individual in an oppressive environment. "One of the most critical and unavoidable stages of being trapped," I read, "is when a person begins to blend into his surroundings. When, spurred on by his delirium, he envisions an imaginary flight." One doesn't have to be a mountaineer to dream of fleeing beyond the Venezuelan peaks. More and more people have this dream every day.

*

My hotel is tall, really tall. More than twenty stories, with waiters, bellhops, cleaning people, receptionists. At first everything seems under control. But then one feels something is lacking. What? Hotel guests. That's it. There's nobody in this hotel. Hundreds of empty rooms. The elevators are stationary. The bar is deserted. None of the employees seem to notice. Housekeeping moves through the halls as if nothing was wrong. They enter and leave rooms that don't show any signs of occupation. What are they cleaning? For whom?

*

Traffic in Caracas. Caracas as traffic. The gridlock of Caracas. The Caracas of gridlock.

*

In Caracas a person doesn't walk. Or walks in fear. Or walks fearlessly and doesn't say anything. They.

*

The president changed the name of the country, which is now called the Bolivarian Republic of Venezuela. In order for a country to grow, it's important to elongate its name. He also changed the time zone, which is now unique in Latin America. The flag was modified: a star added, so now there are eight rather than seven. It was, we might say, a stellar addition. The national coat of arms met the same fate. Its indomitable horse, which looks a lot like the Ferrari logo, changed direction and course. Now everything fits. It's exactly as it should be. Those who look at the coat of arms see a swift gallop to the left while, logically, the administration's horse moves quickly to its right.

*

I flip through the hilarious volume *Anécdotas de una sueño revolucionario* by the artist Weil, who works for *Tal Cual*. The editor of the paper, Teodoro Petkoff, was a militant guerrilla, founded the socialist party MAS, and today is one of the biggest opponents of the government. As punishment for a satirical article, the paper received an enormous fine that would have forced them to shut down had they not pooled together a collection to defray the cost. Soon after, Weil's caricatures of Chávez began to appear with a jackboot over the president's head, hiding his face, and through which he continues to deliver his speeches.

*

I make some inquiries about my hotel. Its previous name was The Four Seasons. It faces Altamira Plaza. This is where soldiers loyal to Pedro Carmona, the fleeting interim president who illegally overthrew Chávez and had no better plan than to abolish the Constitution, set up a barricade. Civilians and opposition leaders also camped here. There were rallies, demonstrations, and, according to believers, the virgin of the plaza cried anti-Chávez tears. There were disturbances and an assassination. The hotel was the place where dissident leaders could meet and rest. When the revolt ended, the owners were forced to close the hotel under pressure from the government. The building was put up for sale. It changed hands. It remained inactive for several years. It reopened. And then I arrived. The first guest? The concierge looks at me with a vampiric smile.

*

The filmmaker Spike Lee is visiting the country. The government has invited him to the Villa del Cine, a small revolutionary Hollywood.

"That guy," someone says, "was a chavista before Chávez." Sean Penn, Kevin Spacey, and Tim Robbins have also come to see Venezuelan reality up close. They stayed in the most expensive neighborhoods. They didn't meet with the opposition. They talked to the president for hours and then went on his TV show.

*

Chávez spends tens of hours a week on his show. He governs by TV. A Revolutionary Big Brother. In this sense, you could say he's the most modern president in the world.

*

We get drinks in the San Ignacio mall. I'm told it's very safe at night: there are armed guards and private parking. Before allowing us through the checkpoint, they search our bags with a flashlight and emphatically pat down our waists. "*Salud*," the waiter smiles.

*

Deposed President Zelaya, flanked by cameras, advances toward Honduras, triumphantly crosses the border, sees the government's military forces, and then prudently retreats.

*

Japan floods. Spain burns. It hails in Iowa. I turn off the TV. It gets dark.

*

Aha. I find out that last month Vargas Llosa stayed in my hotel, my empty hotel, when he came for a series of conferences about democratic liberties. I am told there were demonstrations and protests in the plaza across the street. On the hotel door there's a sticker I hadn't yet noticed. It's from the Ministry of Popular Power for Tourism. It says, "Offender."

*

Despite everything—and this is the exciting thing, this is why I find this country so admirable—Venezuelan literature grows. "Go figure," a friend comments. "Maybe it's because of the government, or because people need to explain the situation, or to escape, but for whatever reason, more people are writing here than ever."

*

I return to some lines of the poet and narrator Gabriel Jiménez Emán's *Baladas profanas*. In one of the poems, I read, "The trash heap of time / . . . the days that disappear leaving behind / stories piled high / stories that grind into one another / and that make plans beneath this tree / with the only goal of being alone / with me."

*

The book's aim is formulated at the beginning: "Again, a hole in the wall / to see, to see."

*

Throughout the entire week, I say, I haven't met a single intellectual in favor of Chávez. "I don't think," someone responds, "you can be both things at the same time."

*

127

Caracas airport. Entrance. An enormous sign: "If you're with Movistar, you're in everywhere." Everything in Movistar, nothing outside of the revolution. Who copies whom?

*

Boarding is my last Bolivarian experience. I go to pay the fees. At the window they ask me for 140 bolívares or the equivalent in foreign currency at the fictitious exchange rate set by the government. It would be difficult for a foreigner to carry that many bolívares just before leaving. So the majority of us shell out seventy dollars rather than the eighteen or nineteen we actually owe. As far as I can tell, it's the highest airport fee in the world. I look at my wallet. I have only twenty euros. I leave the line and search for an ATM. As I walk down the hallway, three luggage wrappers approach me in turn. They are all in official uniforms and they all offer me bolívares. I say no to the first two. On the third try, I realize they're proposing a deal. A swindle to match the other swindle. If I use the ATM, the Venezuelan banking network will give me just over three bolívares for each of my euros. I'll have to withdraw forty-five euros. In hushed tones, the luggage wrapper offers me four bolívares per euro. Now we're negotiating. I do it with conflicted emotions. I tell him that both he and I know that one euro is really worth more than ten bolívares. That I have twenty euros. That all this seems like a rip-off to me. He laughs, and deep down, I do, too. He raises his offer to five bolívares. I tell him no, thanks. "Six," he says. Have a good day, I respond. Then he stops me: "Give me the twenty euros and I'll pay the fee." I calculate mentally. He's offering me seven bolívares per euro. I accept with a sigh. I give him my money. And he immediately gives me a roll of bills, the exact amount of the airport fee. This was the protocol, not what's happening at the window. I make my way to the window.

*

On the cover of *El Nacional* I read, "The head of state demanded that the Assembly revive the constituent power. The president claimed that the process is changing and will end when the structures of the bourgeois state have been removed." The issue remains what to do with Them.

10

Bogotá, What a Shame about Congress

AS SOON AS I SET FOOT in the Bogotá airport, I remember what it's like to be in the Bogotá airport. After long, slow lines, you have to pass through two consecutive luggage checks. Even if you're just stopping over. Soldiers in green inspect your belongings. Some have multiple decorations. One of them messes up my dirty laundry with a mixture of disgust and surgical precision. He has trouble closing my suitcase. He forces it. And breaks off the zipper tab. When he finally manages to close it, another official pats me down. As people tend to do during the pat-down, I shift my gaze to the side. And then I see another official waving two huge wooden needles, like a Chinese diner the size of Gulliver. He perforates a bag that a woman had in her suitcase. He sinks the needles in deep, trying to touch the bottom. He extracts them carefully, an airport bullfighter. He lifts the needles to his nose. He breathes in. Closes his eyes. And nods, coming out of the trance. I'm ashamed to have taken so long to understand what he was doing.

*

When I arrive, as always, it's raining and it's not. The weather in this beloved city is a perpetual homage to ambiguity. "If you don't like the weather in Bogotá," they say, "wait five minutes."

*

HOTEL IN BOGOTÁ: BH El Retiro.
HOTEL ENVIRONMENT: Sophisticated Discomfort.
RECEPTION STYLE: A Very un-Colombian Coldness.

*

I pick up the phone and ask how to turn up the heat. Amazingly, the receptionist answers that in Bogotá there's no heating. And she adds that in this hotel "one regulates one's own temperature by opening or closing the window." Or waiting five minutes, right?

*

I stay in the residential zone of El Retiro, very different from the chaotic and threatening Bogotá. We walk through the beautiful Usaquén neighborhood, enjoying the happy colors and flea market. We end up eating—of all things—Spanish tapas in a restaurant called Sepúlveda. At this point in the journey, I celebrate it as a return.

*

At the next table various Spanish diners are having lunch. Suddenly, from my "Colombian" perspective, I find them (us) rude, loud, and hyper. They speak (we speak) as if trying to convince everyone else. I don't find it all that convincing.

*

An impersonator from the radio show *La Luciérnaga* arrives at the restaurant. She is pleasant and eats a lot, as if each of her voices demands a meal. She relates a conversation she once had with former

Colombian president Rafael Uribe. "Are you the person who tells those little fables?" the president asked her. "No, I tell jokes. You're the one who tells little fables."

*

We start to talk about machismo. A woman from Bogotá, in a spectacular act of self-deception, says something I've heard before: in Spain there is more machismo than in other countries, because there's more news about abused women. I ask her how many cases have been reported here. What official data exists. She shrugs.

*

"He didn't plan on penetrating her," I read in a story by Pilar Quintana. "He was just going to rub up against her until he came. As he was doing that the girl's breathing quickened, she was clearly awake and she wasn't resisting. So he lied to himself by saying he was only going to put in the tip. When he did, the girl let out a moan. It seemed to him like a sound of pleasure and he could no longer contain himself."

*

I read *Las fantásticas*, compiled from the testimonies of ex-wives and former girlfriends of drug dealers. It's edited by the journalist Juan Camilo Ferrand of Bogotá and former narco Andrés Lopéz of Cali, who turned himself in to the US justice system and from his jail cell wrote the best-selling book *El cartel de los sapos*, later made into a popular television series. In the prologue, the authors state their intention of making "a desperate call to all of the young women of Colombia" to avoid wasting their youth "with criminals in exchange for a bit of money and fun" and to find their own path, which "if it might be more difficult in comparison with the easiness [sic] which comes from being beside a drug dealer, also is much more satisfying and good for the soul." Grammar aside, it bothers me that the book assumes that sleeping with narcos is easier and more comfortable than studying and working. It also seems strange that female independence is depicted almost as a sacrifice, whose benefits are limited to the soul. The epilogue does mention economic independence in passing, though mainly as a warning to "those young girls that still dream of conquering a drug dealer" not only because of a lack of money but also because of "laziness and lack of motivation." As happens in the courts, some defenses seem like accusations. The general working conditions of women don't enter into their analysis. One of the women says, concretely, "We couldn't afford any luxuries because my dad didn't give us anything . . . and my mom had to find ways to make ends meet." Later she summarizes her parents' relationship: "Sundays were the best days. From Monday to Thursday they didn't speak, on Friday [my father] beat her and on Saturday she got down on her knees to pray." "But if this dynamic continued," the didactic authors maintain, "it's because the relationship was loving."

*

"There's a rule with the FARC kidnappings," someone says. "Whoever returns from captivity publishes a book. In that book, they insult other prisoners even more than the abductors."

*

The Colombian army uses an incentive system that compensates soldiers for every casualty in the guerrilla forces. This system has led to the practice of the "false positive," which consists of murdering poor young men and then exhibiting their corpses in guerrilla garb. The Attorney General's Office is currently investigating (can it?) some two thousand cases of false positives. Almost 30 percent of the members of Congress, most of them aligned with the government, have been prosecuted for their suspected links to paramilitary groups. Borges believed that democracy relied too much on statistics. But many democrats create unreliable statistics.

*

I read Ricardo Silva's *Autogol*. It tells the story of an announcer who lost his voice when the Colombian defender Andrés Escobar accidentally scored an own goal during the fateful match against the United States in the '94 World Cup, leading to his assassination a few days later. The novel moves from soccer to politics. In "Second Half," a famous paramilitary soldier, who has rubbed elbows with the most important businessmen and politicians in the country, asserts, "I trust the capos much more than the politicians. I'll have you know that the only people who stabbed me in the back were those señores from Bogotá living on a cloud." "All businessmen," the narrator comments, "risk their lives to make money." The difference is that illegal businessmen "tended to fall into the traps the politicians set for them. They allowed themselves to be seduced by the title of 'doctor,' by the chance to discuss Colombian history, by the honor of receiving candidates with important last names in their fancy living rooms. They financed campaigns. . . . And then, when they became a liability to prestige, they were thrown away like old spouses. Hadn't the same thing happened to the bandits in the era of violence? Hadn't they turned in their weapons only to shoulder the blame during the peace accords?"

*

What's the traffic like in Bogotá? A sign inside a taxi gives an admirable summary: "Demand that your driver follow the rules of the road! . . . Respect for traffic lights and everything else. If you don't protest or complain, your life is in danger." The most disturbing thing is that "and everything else."

*

Andalusia and Colombia are two places with *shame*. They both refer to shame as an archetypal sentiment, though in two different senses. In Andalusia shame is an intimate and almost inherited tragedy associated with fate. In Colombia shame is a daily reserve before the other, for the other. Andalusian people are born with private shame and live to communicate it to others. Colombian people learn to feel shame, develop it as a social faculty. The strange thing is that, though Andalusian shame is much worse, its folklore imitates, exalts, and almost loves this pain ("My shame, little shame, my little shame"), while Colombian courtesy requires one to disavow it as much as possible ("Oh, I'm sorry, what a shame!").

*

I notice that the overvaluation and exploitation of nonfiction (literature that is not only interesting but also much easier to get published) is beginning to wear on people. "Literature," Juan David Correa reminds us in *El Malpensante* magazine, "should appeal to language, character, and imagination, since that's where its power resides." Not coincidentally, in another essay in the same issue, Luis Fernando Afanador writes, "The time has come to raise our voices to say to the four winds that, even if it is true that the genre of the novel is impure and doesn't have fixed rules . . . not just any text is a novel. . . . We have to recognize that best sellers sometimes have superior qualities to certain works that disguise themselves as experimental."

*

They take me to meet former president Belisario Betancur, who governed Colombia when I was starting school. At the age of eighty-six, he preserves his happy demeanor and his energy. He wears a (literally) stellar tie: moon and stars against a black background. His shiny nails, meticulously manicured, catch my gaze. The windows of his office are foggy, which prevents us from looking outside. These days Señor Betancur heads the Santillana Foundation, where everyone calls him *Presidente*, though it's unclear whether they're referring to his current role or his former position. He has written numerous essays on politics, education, and the economy, in addition to stories such as *Media vuelta a la derecha*. On his desk I catch a glimpse of two books: *La pasión de gobernar* and *La penitencia del poder*, the "penitence of power" being a phrase that García Márquez used to refer to Betancur's literary vocation. Señor Betancur is playful and a storyteller. He embellishes his convictions with anecdotes. He reminds me of a phrase by Álvaro Mutis: "Poetry always dresses in a suit and tie, not in a guayabera." I'm afraid I've never been dressed for poetry. During our conversation, Señor Betancur mentions last names that appear with equal frequency in Colombian politics and culture. Perhaps García Márquez's masterpiece is a magical saga because that's the way national history has been constructed: genealogically, circularly.

*

I walk, or better yet climb, the Candelaria neighborhood. These hills are a combination of colonial past and university-age youth. Bars, cultural centers, restaurants, theaters, and the good-bad life are on display all over. Here it's easy to feel like one is a native of Bogotá.

*

At night, just like in Venezuela, everybody goes out dancing. Do they go out to dance? Or do they dance to go out?

*

In *Sin remedio*, Antonio Caballero's now-classic novel, which reads like a Colombian-style *Hopscotch*, I read the following dialogue: "—How have the Bogotá nights treated you? I saw you dancing real close, doin' your thing. —Ay, Escobar, don't be silly. The guy was trying to grab me, and I was trying to keep him away, blocking him with my elbow. But the guy was really strong, and he was pushing up against me with his belly! And you know what? He had an enormous pistol in his pants. I was terrified. —Maybe it wasn't a pistol. —Ay, don't be silly! He's clearly an army intelligence agent."

*

Someone says, "The devil is scarier here in Colombia than anywhere else."

*

I return to the hotel, turn on the TV, and see Televisión Española, the channel that scrupulously selects the worst Spanish shows to disseminate abroad.

*

Home, cruel home. News breaks on the TV about an ETA bomb, another ETA bomb, in Civil Guard residential barracks in Burgos. Thirteen children are wounded. I remember the sympathy that the terrorists from the richest community in the Spanish state elicited (and still elicit?) among certain Latin American progressives. None of these countries will ever enjoy the well-being or the economic privileges of their Basque comrades.

*

Tomorrow I will get up early to go to the airport. Tomorrow, which is already today. To return to the airport. Tomorrow, which was today. I wonder whether I'm coming or going. Today, which is already tomorrow. I wonder whether I've ever left the airport.

*

I return to *El Malpensante*, which has continued to think its dirty thoughts in my unwashed clothes, and I come upon a joke that's just too perfect. "Who's calling me at four in the morning?" asks the Devil, sleeping on one side of the bed. "One of those idiots who wants you to help them just because they get up early," God responds, hanging up the phone on the other side of the bed.

*

As happens in almost every country in Latin America, the taxi driver apologizes for not being able to offer me a seat belt. "People say it's uncomfortable," he explains, while speeding up to sixty miles an hour.

*

"When I flew to Spain," the driver tells me, "they searched everything. They even opened my Alka-Seltzers."

*

And finally, in the Bogotá airport, I'm exempted from paying the very worldly airport fees. What's more, to my surprise, although I've only spent three days in the country, I'm reimbursed seventy thousand pesos. It's the only airport in the entire continent where something like this has happened. I don't know whether to cry, ask for forgiveness, or give back the money.

*

Chávez is literally, physiologically tireless. Today's cover of *El Tiempo* announces, "Chávez withdraws his ambassador and threatens trade relations. Following a polemic about weapons, he advocates for replacing Colombian imports and warns that he could expropriate companies." Facing the newsstand is a bookstand, where, rearing its head, is Jorge Volpi's new essay volume, *El insomnio de Bolívar*. Does Chávez ever sleep?

*

"Swedish weapons in the hands of the FARC," the EFE agency informs. "Tensions increase between Colombia and Venezuela. . . . The Swedish Government confirmed to the Colombian media today that various rocket launchers produced in their country, and recently seized from the Revolutionary Armed Forces of Colombia, had been sold to Venezuela in the late 1980s. . . . The Venezuelan ambassador, Nicolás Maduro, stated today that the government would respond 'at the appropriate time' to 'this new lie.' . . . The trade relationship between Colombia and Venezuela has also suffered in this antagonistic atmosphere, and the committee on bilateral integration predicts that trade between the countries will close the year at five billion dollars, less than the ten billion dollars initially anticipated." They will find a way to compensate for the deficit. With American or Swedish weapons.

*

El Tiempo says that a group of narcos offered to donate fifteen million pesos for the reconstruction of one of the towers of the Manizales basilica. The contribution, "according to official sources," was rejected. Since it's unlikely that the narcos wanted to publicize this rejection, I assume that the Church called the press to brag about having spoken with the drug lords without negotiating with them. It's strange that this isn't taken for granted. The curate Rodrigo López, in his attempt to wash the image of the Virgin Mother, ended up muddying his hands. "They sent one of my very best friends to say that they were willing to finance the restoration of the right wing," he boasted. "But I didn't accept the proposal." Congratulations, Father. You're an expert at resisting temptation.

*

The paper is frankly entertaining. "The greatest survey ever produced in the country," I read, "reveals that television is the new king of domestic appliances, defeating the stove, which was in first place in 2004." What would my hotel receptionist say about this? As a demonstration of Chávez's international discredit, the paper cites declarations from the Israeli chancellor, who has recently arrived in Bogotá: "Chávez speaks a strange language." They haven't chosen the best source. The language that Israel employs in foreign relations isn't exactly Hebrew. More sensibly, a senator from the opposition observes, "The decision to set up US military bases in Colombia was bound to generate reactions in neighboring countries." A sports journalist might call that an own goal. Meanwhile, in Cuba, the Colombian singer Juanes's planned concert in the Plaza de la Revolución still hasn't been approved. "I call upon the authorities," Silvio Rodríguez demands, "to authorize this concert." In regimes like Castro's and Chávez's, everyone ends up giving orders.

*

Just before boarding, I come upon the most interesting advertisement I've ever seen in a Latin American airport. The ad, which initially adopts some of the country's colloquial phrases, is from HSBC: "The more you look at the world, the more you recognize that people value things in different forms. HSBC. The local bank of the world." Globalization had never formulated with such exactitude its own limits and contradictions. A monopoly on diversity. Capital unified by difference. *The local bank of the world.* Sometimes one wants to stop reading the news and start reading advertisements. It's a better way to understand the world.

*

In *The Secret History of Costaguana*, Juan Gabriel Vásquez's novel that recreates the history of Colombia alongside Conrad's biography, I read, "The country that is now called New Granada granted the United States exclusive rights of transit over the Isthmus of the Panama province, and the United States agreed, among other things, to maintain strict neutrality in domestic politics. And here begins the disorder, here begins . . . "

11

Mexico City, Successful Catastrophes

MEXICAN CUSTOMS FORM. A whole lot of show in a colorful two-page form. On the list of objects considered part of your personal luggage you will find: "Clothes, including a bride's trousseau; foot-wear and beauty products, provided they are consistent with the length of your travel," and "a set of hand tools in their case, which may include a drill, clamps, keys, dice, screwdrivers, and electric cables." *México lindo*, marriageable and masculine!

*

Flying over Mexico City, slowly traversing its interminable gray cloud, is the closest thing I've ever known to landing on the moon.

*

I was ready to put down an original thought about the country, when someone from the airport's Duty Free came to offer us tequila in little plastic cups.

*

After Ecuador, the swine-flu mania has substantially subsided. I barely see any masks. Still, the special health notices continue to be distributed in every airport. Here it's simple and clear. The only difference is that they use the informal *tú* form to address the passenger: "*Con el objeto de proteger tu salud, te pedimos que respondas . . .*" The friendliness of this detail makes me feel welcome and somewhat relieved. We tend to think of the government in the formal *usted* form.

*

The casual hospitality of the Mexican airport surprises me. It's as if the fact they had the flu before anyone else has shielded and cured them (from the fear, that is). I walk to the immigration counter. "Hi, how's it going," the official greets me. "Thank you, go ahead, see you later, good luck," he dismisses me. I'm tempted to stay inside the building. I'll ask for a Mexican passenger's passport, or for them to let me pass as a Mexican passenger.

*

HOTEL IN MEXICO CITY: Crowne Plaza.
HOTEL ENVIRONMENT: Wealthy.
RECEPTION STYLE: Bureaucratic, *Güey*.

*

I see a documentary on TV about the history of the Zócalo square. For many years, people thought that dancing was prohibited in the symbolic site, and so no concerts were organized there. When Celia Cruz was invited to inaugurate the first series of massive events in the Zócalo, they discovered that there had never been a law prohibiting it.

*

In Spain summer burns like hell. Another ETA attack. This time in Mallorca. Two members of the Civil Guard, both younger than I am, were killed in a tourist area. Talking with friends, I find out that until very recently, an important national newspaper was openly pro-ETA. According to what they tell me, one of the directors belonged to the group. I don't know if it's true, but it would make sense. It seems more and more obvious that certain types of terrorism, particularly bourgeois terrorism, rely on their image in the media for strength. Less through the ways they present their own positions than through the image they project of their enemies.

*

We pass by Azteca Stadium, on Avenida Viaducto Tlalpan, in the car. Euphoric memories of the 1986 World Cup final, which was played here and fueled the dreams of so many kids who watched it on TV, immediately wash over me. The last time the Argentine national team was truly great. Also, probably the last time that Argentina thought it was great. I look up at a traffic sign: "Transference Station."

*

El Candelero restaurant, in Colonia del Valle, is decorated with virgins, saints, and other religious figures. An angel, looking like a gluttonous canary, is perched in a cage. There are chapels, altarpieces, and cupolas. And, of course, live *ranchera* music. Only in Seville could you find a similar mix of baroque devotion, heretical kitsch, and humor. Enjoy your meal, O divine ones!

*

They put salsa on their salsa.

*

"In this same restaurant," a friend tells me, "I saw the actress María Félix for the last time. The grand dame came in and everyone fell silent. At that moment I recalled that a reporter once asked her if she was a lesbian, and she responded, 'If all men were as ugly as you are, of course I'd be.' Nobody in the restaurant dared to speak to her. They just stared. She had a special presence. Maybe she was already dead."

*

We talk about the anti-Francoist Spanish émigrés who came to Mexico. "When you really think about it," someone says, "Franco created Mexico." Everyone at the table stops chewing.

*

This city is a country. Its delegations are provinces. Its *colonias*, cities. Its avenues, rivers. Without realizing it, when Borges described cartographic madness in "On Exactitude in Science," he envisioned the map of Mexico City.

*

"The equation," I read in Álvaro Enrigue's *Vidas perpendiculares*, "changed when they moved to ferocious Mexico City."

*

Stopped at a traffic light, I see an old man in a wheelchair, his face ravaged, his beard yellowed, his body punished, and his mouth a mass of flesh. He wears a red T-shirt with white letters: "Live to death," it says.

*

Mexico City is a giant mobile radio station. Everyone listens to the radio; nobody gets to their destination; every inhabitant drives a car lost in a sea of cars; nobody knows when they'll get where; it's impossible to read when in traffic; everyone listens to the radio.

*

On the way to the pyramids at Teotihuacán, we take the scary Mexico–Pachuca route. We talk about Ciudad Juárez, about Bolaño, about poor and violent neighborhoods. We go under a sign and I misread it: "*Autopsia de México*," instead of "*Autopista de México*."

*

"When you see an insect run, follow it," I read in *Oscuro bosque oscuro*, Jorge Volpi's hypnotic novel in verse. "When you discover an insect in hiding, denounce it; when an insect asks you for mercy, squash it."

*

Teotihuacán, an architectural mystery. To the best of our knowledge, the greatest pre-Columbian city. I walk between the pyramids. I cross Avenida de los Muertos. The *Teotihuacanos* who lived here were priests and philosophers. They weren't warriors. It was the only time that philosophers ruled priests. Naturally, they disappeared.

*

I shift my eyes from the Pyramid of the Sun, to the east, to the Pyramid of the Moon, to the north. The stone and the greenness converse in a low, deep, distant voice. "This is un-fucking-believable," someone exclaims by my side.

*

The stairs of the Pyramid of the Sun are not as small as had been suggested to me. That's why, on this pyramid, the maxim isn't true that to go down a pyramid, you can never turn your back to the gods. Or maybe the Teotihuacanos had huge feet? I look at the pyramid from below. People pass obliquely over its surface, as if skirting a chiseled cliff. Gravity doesn't exist for the gods of this world. The people up there seem like shadows, points, edges of rock. That's religion.

*

Standing on top of the solar pyramid, I am a weather vane, the center of nothing, a question in the wind.

*

I'm told that every March 21, during the equinox, a crowd dressed in white surrounds this pyramid. The next day the headlines say things like, "A Million People Get Together to Take in Some Light."

*

Our car circles the lake and park of Chapultepec. I think of the painter Ramón Gaya, who went into exile in Mexico after the Spanish Civil War. I think about his subtle series of watercolors of this very lake. Of course, I won't actually see Chapultepec. I travel almost without seeing, I see everything in passing. In a certain way, this seems like an homage to the Spanish-Mexicans of the Republic. Let this omission of a description of Lake Chapultepec, the impossibility of contemplating it, serve as a reminder of what Gaya couldn't see in Spain, of everything he wasn't allowed to see.

*

I read *Hecho en México*, a literary collage compiled by Lolita Bosch, who was born in Barcelona and lived in Mexico City. Antonio Ortuño, who was born in Jalisco and whose parents are Spanish, figures among its authors. "My grandfather was in the Republican army," Ortuño recounts in his author biography, "but because he was a democrat and not a communist nobody considered him a hero." His novel *Recursos humanos* is equally saddening.

*

I see *Temporada de patos*, by Fernando Eimbcke, which reminds me of another first film, the Uruguayan *25 Watts*. In addition to its wonderfully silly humor, the great accomplishment of Eimbcke's film is its static, morose, contemplative narrative, in which all of the characters want to move, change, flee to somewhere else. "Ducks often feel a great need to migrate," the pizza man suggests. "It's not that the duck that migrates is a bad duck, but that his nature makes him migrate. To seek new waters or warmer weather. I don't know. They're ducks."

*

New airport in Mexico City. Waiting for the flight to Monterrey. I'm drinking tea at a table. Light rolls through the hallways. The combination of the tea and the afternoon suddenly gives me great pleasure. This calm in the midst of the bustle, this certainty derived from neither place, nor country, nor cause, which can steal upon us anywhere like the caress of a stranger on the back of the neck, this provisional and perhaps ridiculous happiness, is the most valuable remembrance I'll take from this journey.

*

México lindo, the airport bookstore. The titles on the first shelf, from left to right: *Historias de impunidad*; *Los cómplices del presidente*; *País de mentiras*; *Herencia maldita. El reto de Calderón y el nuevo mapa del narcotráfico*; *Las FARC en México*; *Las historias más negras de narco, impunidad y corrupción en México*; *Los capos. Las narco-rutas de México*; *Crónicas de sangre*; *Los brujos del poder*, and an explosive et cetera. These titles suggest more excitement than indignation toward the crimes, scandals, and catastrophes rocking the country. I'm not sure whether this bibliography is meant to criticize one type of business or to create another.

*

México acribillado by Francisco Martín Moreno is one of the most successful novels of the year. It tells the story of the assassination of President Obregón, who, having just been reelected in 1928, died of gunshot wounds from six different types of bullets—that is, from a half dozen assassins. Either they all experienced a miraculous telepathic connection, or they all received the same instructions from the same bosses. A year after this assassination the PRI was founded, which governed the country for seventy years, with politicians of various calibers.

*

I also find a book by the former minister of education. It's called, *Dios mío, hazme viuda, por favor. El desafío de ser tú misma* (My God, Please Make Me a Widow: The Challenge of Being Yourself).

*

During the flight to Monterrey, where I will spend the day working, I read a magazine published by the bookstore chain Gandhi: *Lee+*. The issue is devoted to ugliness and the myth of beauty. On the cover, Marilyn Monroe appears in full splendor, golden hair and skin, a timeless black-and-white photo. Or not exactly. In a report titled "Ugly people with beautiful words," a quote from the French singer-songwriter Serge Gainsbourg (owner, by the way, of a nose that speaks volumes) declares, "Ugliness has one advantage over beauty: it lasts longer."

*

The report concludes with an absurd assertion that could absolutely be true: "If Jean Paul Sartre hadn't been so ugly, *Being and Nothingness* wouldn't exist." The stewardess, who is very beautiful, instructs me to put my seat in an upright position.

*

Why is it that, when the plane lands, all of the passengers get up as quickly as possible, when we know that we can't deplane for several minutes? Why does this line of impatient people, this immobile herd, wait in the most uncomfortable position for the moment of the stampede? There's something terrible about this rush. We are all going toward death, but we don't know it or don't acknowledge it.

And we do everything possible to cut short the little time we have. I recall a line from Lorca: "The dead moan, waiting for their turn."

*

I land in Monterrey. The heat is so tight there is no longer any difference between the desert and our selves.

*

Monterrey airport. México lindo often surprises me with the openness of its machismo, as open as the young girls that appear in its ads. On a poster for LG cell phones, a model with an unmistakably adolescent air raises her thin white T-shirt to show off her stomach and navel. Tiny shorts don't quite succeed in covering her private parts. The girl is supposedly listening to music on her new phone with Dolby sound, but she doesn't seem to be paying much attention to the headphones. She just stares at the camera with a look of sexual desperation. In case we don't get it, the caption tells us, "Music makes me do it." In one corner of the poster, the company indicates, "Life is good." Really good.

*

My guide to the city is not underage, but she does have a next-generation cell phone. I ask to borrow it to do a search. I enter the phrase "music makes me do it" and I find an article about a dance competition sponsored by the Mexican division of LG, which just launched a line of cell phones with music. The headline: "LG Supports Our Youth."

*

Most Mexican women have small butts, almost as if they'd gotten tired of Mexican men slapping them.

*

I stay in the majestic Ancira Hotel. Right here, between its marble banisters and palatial balustrades, José Doroteo Arango, alias Pancho Villa, opened fire. Right where Bar 1900 sits today, in front of the counter, is where he started shooting and demanding money. I walk to the bar. José Doroteo? With a name like that there was no way to start a revolution like a man.

*

HOTEL IN MONTERREY: Gran Hotel Ancira.
HOTEL ENVIRONMENT: Postrevolutionary Decadence.
RECEPTION STYLE: Enigmatic.

*

I read *Pétalos* by Guadalupe Nettel, who has a gift for describing the repulsive in a sublime way. Or, to evoke one of its stories, for affectionately taking in the rank odors of the bathroom: "In the life of all smellers," the character maintains, "there is a moment of fullness."

*

We dine at the Ambassador Hotel. The area around the restaurant is, in a word, moving. A cupola with stained-glass windows. Plastic palm trees. Embroidered tablecloths. On one of the tables sits an old issue of *El Periódico USA*, printed in McAllen, Texas. I am surprised to find Honduras on the front page of a newspaper from Texas. Another news item appears next to it: "This week

Operation Lone Star began in the Texas valley, bringing quality medical and dental services to the population free of charge. The brigades are made up of military forces." That is what we call chewing the news.

*

The EFE agency informs us, "The Caracas headquarters of the Venezuelan chain Globovisión has been attacked with tear gas by a group identified with the ruling party. . . . Earlier, the president had threatened to close the news channel for practicing 'media terrorism.'" This argument reminds me of Bush. "The government," I continue reading, "has hardened its line against opposition media outlets over the last few weeks. On Saturday, they shut down thirty-four radio stations that have now become the property of the state. Over 250 stations—forty regional TV channels and 210 radio stations—have been threatened with closure for 'trying to brainwash the Venezuelan people.'" This argument reminds me of Freud.

*

On my last night off during the first part of the tour, I'm attacked by a sudden, absurd, and euphoric desire to go to a roulette table and bet all the money I have left. I ask where there's a casino. My friends remind me that Mexican law prohibits gambling. "For that," says one of them, "we already have politics."

*

In bed I read the short story "El huidor," by the wonderful Fabio Morábito. It tells of the adventures of an alternative superhero, a mix of a poet and a delinquent, whose only power consists of running away without having done anything wrong. When they finally catch him, he is unrecognizable. After so much running, his features have blended with his environment. "His face seemed the sum of all faces," the story ends, "as if by the force of flight he had freed himself from any characteristic of his own." I close the book. I go into the bathroom, turn on the light, and have no idea who that guy in front of me is.

*

Against the background of Monterrey, like an overly calculated decoration, the Cerro de la Silla appears, with its exaggerated edges and a silhouette worthy of the Roadrunner cartoons. I don't know if this remarkable hill protects us or warns us of something. I ask this question, in this way, to the driver. "It ignores us," he answers. "It ignores us."

*

"In Monterrey," one of my friends from Mexico City had said, "there are three things to see: a contemporary art museum, a contemporary art museum, and a contemporary art museum. You decide."

*

New, old gridlock in Mexico City. My eyes get lost among so many cars. I have the feeling that at any moment the traffic will completely stop, evening will slowly set in, we'll get out to stretch our legs, and we'll all be like characters in a Mexican version of Cortázar's "The Southern Highway."

*

"I am," I read in Sandra Lorenzano's *Saudades*, "a smuggler of stories."

*

The headline of the newspaper *Milenio* today, August 4: "The Clergy Condemns Police Raid against Narcos during Mass." Although the police didn't fire a single shot while carrying out the operation (news in itself), the episcopacy considered the successful intervention in Michoacán "a profanation" and "an offense." The Church doesn't like the public to be distracted. The arrested narcos formed part of a group that calls itself La Familia.

*

We talk about Mateo Gil's abandoned film adaptation of *Pedro Páramo*, which was going to feature Gael García Bernal. Apparently there were issues between Spain and Mexico when it came time to make the film. "The Rulfo family," someone says, "speaks in murmurs." Spaniards speak by shouting. It's not surprising they wouldn't understand each other.

*

I see an election ad for the Partido Socialista Democrático: "The death penalty makes us all assassins. To counter violence, intelligence." With this admirably enlightened motto, they'll continue to fail in my México lindo.

*

Last interview during the first part of my tour, before returning to Spain for a summer recess. It's scheduled to take place in the extraordinary Universidad del Claustro de Sor Juana. This is the site of the San Jerónimo convent, the one-time home of my beloved baroque poet Sor Juana Inés de la Cruz. The TV interview takes place in the cloister's auditorium, which is called Divine Narcissus. My little nun doesn't stop with her irony, not even dead.

*

I fill out the form to leave Mexico. I read the header: "Immigration Form for Tourists, Transmigrants, Businessmen, or Visiting Consultants." I'm not interested in tourism, I don't know how to do business, and I can't give advice. I'd like to be a transmigrant.

*

"I'm so uneasy with reality," I read in Juan Villoro's book of short stories *The Guilty*, "that I find planes comfortable."

Guatemala City, Bullets and Kites

SECOND PART OF THE TOUR. Madrid. Barajas Airport, Terminal 4-S. A very young, rich, attractive man appears. Then two more. Three. They have an accent I can't quite place: they sound Argentine, but not exactly. A fourth arrives, and I recognize him. It's Diego Forlán, the Uruguayan forward from Atlético de Madrid. He's waiting with his teammates for a flight that will take them by way of Guatemala to the playoff match with Costa Rica for a spot in the World Cup. Forlán wears jeans, a white T-shirt, a blue pullover, and tennis shoes. Though he's past thirty, he looks like he just graduated from high school. He's not as tall as I thought he'd be. He talks of the qualifying match with Costa Rica and last night's defeat by Real Madrid. "The stupid goalie," he complains in a low voice, while I pretend not to listen, "hid beneath the goalposts." "And that stuff with the black guy," he adds, referring to the Colombian central defender Perea, "is unbelievable. Seriously, you can't give it to him." His teammates laugh. Another blond player with a Beckham-like outfit ("He looks like a gigolo," they joke when he gets there) makes fun of one of the injured Costa Rican players, insinuating that nobody knows who he is. Another player warns him, "Let's not underestimate them."

*

I read declarations from the former German Chancellor Kohl in *El País* on the twentieth anniversary of the fall of the Berlin Wall: "Only Felipe was on our side." Without even thinking, I initially assume he is talking about the Prince of Asturias. Then I realize he's referring to former Spanish Prime Minister Felipe González. All of this seems symptomatic: that my memory had shelved the socialist leader, and that the newspaper would continue to mention him nostalgically on the front page by his first name. I turn the newspaper over. On the back page, they interview the Basque writer Kirmen Uribe, winner of the National Prize in Fiction. "Don't tell me you refuse to grow up," the reporter says. "The truth," answers Uribe, who has the same last name as the Colombian president, "is that I started writing to avoid the adult world, to continue being a bit adolescent." "Adolescents," the reporter objects, "don't have much of a handle on things." "Neither do I," the writer replies.

*

Honduras, like Paris, never ends. The dialogue between Zelaya and Micheletti, who earlier seemed to be on the cusp of an agreement to form a unity government, has failed. It's worth reminding ourselves that they belong to the same party. Four months have passed since the coup. Micheletti swore to the members of the international commission ("with his hand over his heart," the press specifies) that he was willing to give up power as long as it wasn't to Zelaya. The commissioners turned pale, because a few hours earlier Zelaya had made it clear to them that he wouldn't support any unity government he didn't lead. Micheletti never thought of the country's democratic institutions. And Zelaya stopped thinking about his country long ago when he became obsessed with his own legend.

*

The captain announces that he will take an alternative route to avoid the stormy weather that shook the plane on the flight into Madrid. I can't imagine how that flight was, because this one is already awful. The aircraft spasms every twenty seconds. It jolts like a truck on a rocky mountain road. The flight attendants instruct us to stay in our seats. I poke my head out and catch a glimpse of Forlán. He's sleeping with his arm over his forehead, in a dramatic pose, perhaps dreaming of another storm of Costa Rican goals raining down.

*

Before starting our descent into Guatemala, the captain announces that we will fly over Honduras instead of Nicaragua. Paradoxically, this is how we avoid turbulence.

*

From my window I see nothing but great mountains with almost no signs of development. In some countries nature is a necessary luxury. In others, a fatality that everyone tries to escape.

*

In the Guatemalan customs declaration they ask for the following information: first name, middle name, first last name, second last name, married name. I don't know what gives me the greatest relief: to have no middle name, to be a man, or to be unmarried.

*

HOTEL IN GUATEMALA CITY: Barceló.
HOTEL ENVIRONMENT: Wounded Pride.
RECEPTION STYLE: Contemplative.

*

In *Moneda*, the Central American financial newspaper, I read a surprising (or not so surprising) bit of information: "Sales of Honduran Sugar Triple." The paper gives an innocent and partially false reason: an increase in price. Last year, Honduras exported some 160 million pounds for twenty-one million dollars. This year, around 220 million pounds for thirty-four million dollars. In other words, not only have sales increased by over 50 percent, but production has also increased by almost 40 percent. "Despite the global economic crisis and the political situation in Honduras," I continue reading, "the sugar industry has managed to triple its sales on the world market." Despite the political situation? "The greatest share of the sugar," the paper explains without explanation, "has been sold on the US market." Sweet, sugary dreams to you, my dear exporters.

*

Guatemala lives between rains. It rains hard for a bit, then stops, then rains again. I have forgotten my umbrella in my room and start back for it, but he stops me with a knowing smile. "You don't need an umbrella," he says. "You won't use it. In Guatemala you don't walk." I nod and sigh. Storm clouds cover half a continent.

*

In front of my hotel there is a McDonald's and an Ashkenazi synagogue. I try to visit the synagogue, but they don't let me in. To enter you have to pay a fee. I try my luck at the McDonald's.

*

We drink Gallo beer, "famous since 1886," according to the label, "the pride and tradition of Guatemala." We drink to health, everyone's health. And to ward off Hurricane Ida, which just devastated Nicaragua.

*

We order pizza by the meter. Yes. By the meter. We order half a square meter of pizza with pesto. In Guatemala every meter has a price. And a flavor.

*

The level of criminal impunity here is 98 percent. No institution seems reliable, and gangs and mafias, organized territorially, hold the real power. On the drug route, Guatemala forms the bridge between Colombia and the United States. There have been fifty years of internal wars. "Here there's a wall of ice," my friend says, "that numbs you and keeps numbing you."

*

"My nephews," a friend tells me, "came with me to New York for the first time. I had to show them how to cross the street. They didn't know how to do it."

*

On the street I notice something strange. At first I don't know what it is. Suddenly I realize: nobody talks on their phone. And if a cell phone rings outside, nobody answers it.

*

A certain self-destructive steam blends in with the humidity.

*

The lobby of my hotel is filled with doubly antique furniture. That is, furniture made more than thirty years ago that imitates a classic style. As I savor the excellent local coffee, I pause in contemplation, and one piece in particular catches my attention. It's a double throne raised like a chair for church authorities, made of hardwood and covered in purple leather, with four smaller platforms. These platforms give the impression of being absurd pedals, as if the seat were waiting for a driver. It takes me a minute to recognize that it's a luxury piece for shining shoes.

*

It rains. It rains with a green, sticky, indifferent insistence. Our shoes seem like fruits of the land. We take refuge in the car, the true home of all Guatemalan inhabitants. The next morning, the news reports that the downpour has caused a landslide in a nearby town, destroying a hundred homes. My shoes dry comfortably in the sun on the balcony of my room.

*

When the sun appears, the air suddenly changes. We search for our dark glasses. And we look confusedly at the sky, like we always do when we look at the sky.

*

At least half the population is indigenous. The other half is called *ladinos*. When an indigenous person takes off the *corte*, the indigenous dress, he says he's going out ladino-style. Ethnicity is a difficult outfit to shed.

*

There are twenty pre-Hispanic languages in Guatemala. At least a few of them are nearly extinct. Garífuna comes from the black people who came as slaves across the Atlantic. Kaqchikel is the most widely spoken. And Quiché is the most fortunate, since it's the one that Rigoberta Menchú and the poet Humberto Ak'abal speak.

*

I read Humberto Ak'abal. Once I heard him live in Madrid (the word "live" has never been more appropriate: Ak'abal sings, rattles, and rains down his verses in a trance that sounds like a meeting of birds and rivers), but I had never seen one of his books. His poetry is a conversation with pre-Columbian culture, Western literature, and Buddhist perceptions. In *La danza del espanto* I find a Platonic science-fiction idea: "We are born with the memory of the future." Later I read, "Distance is a key: / it opens or closes."

*

On the road to Antigua Guatemala, we cross paths with an ad along Calzada Roosevelt: "Mark Cinema. Digital 3D. Diabolical Temptation—I'll Always Love You—Michael Jackson."

*

"Needless to say, we're getting better," she proudly affirms. "Now we have books in supermarkets."

*

In Antigua, the beautiful capital of the colonial kingdom, I see a blond indigenous woman, old, half cross-eyed, lost. Then I learn that in the country's interior there are many albino indigenous people, particularly women. They almost all die young (younger), segregated from their own people and with skin diseases. Albino Indians: the very essence of the Guatemalan population.

*

In the background the Agua Volcano rises: imperial and lost in the mist. In the mid-sixteenth century it filled with rain and overflowed like a big bucket of water or a lunar drain. That same flood caused the death of the wife of Pedro de Alvarado, Hernán Cortés's military governor and the conqueror of Guatemala. The ironies of nature.

*

1545: The Saint Joseph Cathedral was built. 1668: Demolition of the old cathedral. 1680: The new cathedral is built.1773: Our Lord unleashes an earthquake that destroys it almost completely. 2009: We tourists pay to marvel at its deserted naves, the emptiness of its cupolas, the magnificent emptiness of divine work.

*

At the end of the cathedral is the chapel of the kings, with a Christ in front of which people leave candles, notes, trinkets, quetzals, and dollars. Because of the smoke, like a slow ethnic vengeance, Christ's skin gradually darkens.

*

Antigua is located in the Panchoy Valley, which runs through the Pensive River. As one would expect, it is not a fast-running river.

*

We stop to eat at the Posada de Don Rodrigo, a complex of colonial buildings with separate fountains, small gardens, and stones that have seen much. One of the rooms is called the Posada of Eternal Love. They say that whoever sets foot in it must deal with the consequences. I walk in and out thinking of you.

*

In Tanque de la Unión, a rectangular plaza surrounded by palm trees that seem out of place in this climate, there are public washbasins. Indigenous women still come to the basins to wash their clothes by hand every morning, as they've been doing for centuries. "Parts of Guatemala," a friend remarks, "are doors to the past."

*

A bulletin board on the fifth street, west corner: "Funeral contracts at a good price. For information call 43473 . . . or 52748 . . . "

*

Are there many tourists? Let's give an example. In the Rainbow Café, in the delicious Antigua historical district, they sell used books. I look around. Almost all the copies are in English. Including the Popol Vuh, "the Mayan book of the dawn of life and the glories of gods and kings," and *An Indian Woman in Guatemala*, by Rigoberta Menchú. A book that, from the looks of it, nobody cares to read in Spanish.

*

Sixth avenue north. Kafka bar and hostel. A sign by the entrance: "Premier League soccer!! Liverpool vs. Birmingham, 3:00 p.m." We go in to ask why the place is called Kafka. "He's a Swedish writer the owner likes a lot," a waitress diligently explains.

*

I laugh while reading *Helarte de la errata*, by the Guatemalan narrator Carlos López, a compilation of literary misunderstandings and verbal rarities. The second chapter is called "*¡Gora Euskadi Askatutá!* The ETA came without errata." The fifth chapter is called "*¿Eh, rata?*" Reading the book I discover that "in Guatemala there's a cantina called La Mezquita (the mosque), that some people, without a drop of alcohol in their systems, pronounce La Mosquita (the fly)." Naturally, the last sentence in the book is a sequence of typos and transpositions: "*El ciudado de la eidción estvuo a crgao de Clroas Lpóez.*"

*

This morning, in Zone 10, they shot up a tourist bus. We pass by in our car. I catch sight of a police van and various inspectors studying the scene. "Since the bus was empty," someone offers, "it seems clear that this was just an act of intimidation." Well, in my case, I say, it worked very well.

*

One—another—woman killed. She was stoned to death in the department of Izabal. The radio announcer defines it as "intrafamily violence." The expression seems more appropriate than "domestic violence," which emphasizes the housework attributed to the victim.

The family, it's true, is generally messed up. But at the same time I find the term too general, more disguised than "gender violence," which identifies the problem better. Do some aunts hit their nephews for the same reason that so many men hit their wives?

*

On the website Libros Mínimos, a space devoted to disseminating the work of young Central American authors, I read a poem by Alejandra Flores: "Years ago / I was / scared of everything, / now all that's / left / is the fear of killing you." Later I linger over a microstory by Javier Payeras that begins, "The girl continued to shed layers until she completely disappeared."

*

On the seventh avenue of Zone 1, an inflamed horde of men in shirts rush after our car, waving their arms, pounding the windows, and grabbing the rearview mirrors. I ask the others what these people want so desperately. "To sell us narco-dollars," they answer.

*

In Plaza Mayor, across from the Metropolitan Cathedral and the National Palace, amid parishioners and ice vendors, several former employees of the Agua Pura Salvavidas corporation have been camped out for months. According to their accusations (which would make the name truly ironic), the company has funneled money to different shadow corporations in order to declare bankruptcy and has refused to compensate dozens of fired employees. "Revolution is not celebration," one of their posters claims. "This government pretends to be revolutionary but serves the exploitative bourgeoisie." I walk toward the encampment. "Entry prohibited to capitalists," another poster warns. I leave, just in case.

*

I enter the white, luminous, well-conserved cathedral. On a bulletin board, I read, "You do not need a cell phone to speak to God. Please turn it off."

*

"For more information about our cathedral and its pastoral activities, visit OUR NEW INTERNET SITE. *www.catedralorg.gt."*

*

This cathedral, like many others in Central America, is much more welcoming and warm than those in Spain. Signs indicate rules in a courteous way. The interior is designed to receive you, rather than to intimidate you. Not even the confessionals are hermetic. More than the fear of God, this temple arouses the happiness of Man.

*

The cathedral closes for lunch. "A Spaniard?" the guard asks. Sort of, I answer. "My father was Spanish. From Salamanca," he says. Salamanca is very pretty, I say. "But now Spain is in a really bad way, no?" says the guard. "There are too many immigrants, especially Africans."

*

Walking through the central market, I am immersed in a festival of smells, sounds, colors, leathery faces, and deep life. Here fruit is sold by hand, not by the pound. At a stand for natural products I buy a Here Money Soap. And a Go Away Envy and Evil Neighbors Incense. And an I'm in Charge of My Man Lotion, to give to one of my strong female friends.

*

Esto no es una pipa, the first book by Eduardo Halfon, who was educated in English and writes in Spanish, begins with a Salman Rushdie quote: "To understand just one life you have to swallow the world." In his second book, *Saturno*, a mix of Kafka and Mann, I read, "To speak at someone, Father, is not to speak to them."

*

A friend produces a book by David Foster Wallace. As I flip through it, he says, "It's very badly translated." I ask him why. "Because it sounds like it was written in Spain," he answers, in the name of an entire continent.

*

CHIMAR.
  (from náhuatl *xima*, to shave)
  3. *Coloq. Salvador, Honduras, Nicaragua, Mexico, Guatemala:* To engage in coitus.
  Synonyms: Latin America: to screw, to fuck, to bang.
  Synonyms: Spain: follar, joder, cepillar, tirar.

*

Clásicos El Buki distributes pirated movies. Films that are rarely shown in Guatemala can be found in their store on Sixth Avenue. El

Buki even offers a bulletin of new titles to its subscribers. "Piracy," someone says, "has brought world cinema to this country."

*

On Avenida Reforma there's a sculpture of Miguel Ángel Asturias. The famous writer is standing, holding two large volumes by their spines. Meanwhile, the downward-facing books are losing their brass pages as if they were almanacs. Or were losing them. Or lost them. A few years ago, someone ripped out and stole the pages by Asturias, the Guatemalan Nobel Prize winner.

*

In Guatemala, in November, there is always wind—a swift, impatient wind that seems to want to leave. Weekends, today for example, kids go out with their kites, run while carrying them, hoist them as if they were holding up the future.

*

The airport runway is too short. Large airplanes, lighter at the end of the flight, can make a tight landing, but cannot take off. This means that there are no direct transatlantic flights from here. Guatemala is a mountainous labyrinth, a port for tourists, a wall for its own people.

13

Tegucigalpa, What I Couldn't See

HONDURAS:
MICHELETTI DECLARES STATE OF SIEGE

Tegucigalpa-EFE Agency, 09/27/2009

Honduras's de facto government suspended constitutional guarantees for forty-five days, issuing a decree restricting freedom of movement and speech and prohibiting public meetings. The measures were announced on national radio and television networks. The decree calls for the immediate evacuation of all public institutions occupied by protesters, the closure of all news media outlets that "offend human dignity and public officials or attack the law," and the arrest of all suspicious persons. The measures were taken, according to the decree, in order "to guarantee peace and public order in the country" after the deposed president, Manuel Zelaya, returned to the country in the wake of his removal. . . . At the same time, Micheletti's government gave Brazil a ten-day ultimatum to determine the status of Zelaya, who has taken refuge in the country's embassy. . . . In the same communiqué, Honduran authorities also signaled that they would not allow the return of the Argentine, Spanish, Mexican, or Venezuelan ambassadors, who were removed after the coup of June 28, unless those countries recognize the de facto government. In response, Zelaya has called upon his supporters to redouble their efforts and initiate a "final offensive" to restore him to office. "I'm making a patriotic call to all Hondurans to mobilize and to all those who are able to come to Tegucigalpa for a final offensive," he stated. . . . The measures could further isolate the impoverished Central American nation. It has also destroyed all hopes for dialogue.

*

—Hi, Andrés?

—Yes?

—Can you hear me?

—Kind of, I don't have good service here.

—It's Asun.

—What?

—Asun, from the publishing house.

—Now I hear you, sorry. Hi, Asun.

—How are you?

—Good, you?

—Not bad. I'm calling about the stuff that's happening in Tegucigalpa.

—What?

—Tegucigalpa. Can you hear me? I don't know if you've seen the news.

—Yes, yes, I hear you. I was going to call. What should we do?

—What do you think?

—If it were up to me, I'd go. What do you think?

—Well, it couldn't be a worse time, no?

—Yeah. Or a better time, depending.

—What?

—Can you hear me?

—I hear you fine. Are you sure about that?

—Yes. Well, no. I don't know. If I go, I could take notes on every-thing I see.

—True. But aren't you writing about what you aren't seeing?

—That's a good point. What's the word in the country?

—There's no guarantee that they won't close the borders, airports, or anything else.

—That's not good.

—That's why we think it would be best to cancel.

—I understand. It's a shame. Thanks for your help.

—This is my job, man.

—So you're just saying this because you have to?

—Don't be silly.

—Right. Thanks.

—No problem.

—What? What did you say?

—Can you hear me?

—Hello? Hello?

—Andrés?

—Asun...?

*

LULA CLAIMS THAT OBAMA IGNORES LATIN AMERICA

São Paulo—*Valor*, 11/06/2009

Lula criticized the installation of a US military base in Colombia, and stated that the base should be restricted to the territory within the designated nation, without engaging in activities "along other countries' borders." . . . An editor at the *Financial Times* remarked that the Americans were worried about Venezuela, and asked Lula if he had any advice to give them. "I don't know whether the Americans should be worried about Chávez, or Chávez about the Americans. Each side validates the other," the Brazilian president responded. Lula stated that the Summit of the Americas in Trinidad and Tobago, which both Obama and Chávez attended . . . was a "wonderful" meeting, but that it ultimately didn't lead anywhere. "After the meeting, I told President Obama he had made the initial push to reestablish a more productive relationship with Latin America. But the fact is that nothing has happened since, except for the coup in Honduras," he commented.

*

HONDURAS GOES DOWN THE PATH OF NO RETURN

Tegucigalpa—*El País*, 11/07/2009

Four months and eight days after the coup, Honduras remains the same, only more isolated. Roberto Micheletti continues in the post the military granted him and Manuel Zelaya is still on the sidelines, holed up in the Brazilian Embassy. But the country, which garnered unprecedented international support on June 28, now seems to have been abandoned to its fate, since the agreement between the representatives of Zelaya and Micheletti broke down on Thursday night. At fifty-six years old, Manuel Zelaya is the son of a landowner from Olancho, a violent department in the center of the country composed mainly of farming country. He abandoned his studies in industrial engineering when his father was jailed for an incident involving several dead workers and took over the family farm. . . . Roberto Micheletti, sixty-one years old, went to jail for supporting President Ramón Villeda, overthrown by a coup in 1963. He belongs to the Liberal Party, along with Zelaya, his erstwhile political ally. They turned against each other when Micheletti lost the party's primary for the presidential elections scheduled for later this year.

*

TEGUCIGALPA, WITHOUT HOPE

Tegucigalpa—*El País*, 11/07/2009

Before the coup . . . Ángel David's prospects were not good. He shared eighty-six square feet of a wooden shack with his father, a gardener on strike, and his mother, pregnant with her fifth child, along with his siblings . . . They didn't have a bathroom, because the last storm carried it away, but they did have electricity, a telephone, good manners, and miraculously clean clothes. But then the coup happened and Ángel David's life, never good to begin with, became even worse. His country, the second poorest in Latin America, started to receive sanctions from the international community and 70 percent of its poor . . . became even less well off. . . . That day a rumor spread throughout Honduras that President Manuel Zelaya had secretly managed to return to the country. To celebrate, his supporters organized demonstrations in distinct parts of Tegucigalpa, and Ángel David's father decided to attend. . . . Returning to the house, just after the curfew, they took a shortcut through a side street. They were startled by the sound of a motorcycle approaching them. They looked back. The riders were two policemen. The one behind took aim. . . . The mother, Nelly Rodríguez, invites us into her only room, which is neat and clean, and proudly introduces her children: "My husband and children were walking very slowly, and the policemen could see there were two kids, but they still shot them in the back. The bullet damaged my son's intestines, his colon, his spleen, his liver, and part of his lung. Show the man your scar." Ángel David rises obediently. What did you feel at that moment? "Fear, sir." And anguish? "That, too." And did you lose consciousness? "Yes." What did the anguish feel like? "Like I was going to die." And were you scared? "Yes." Did you cry? "No."

*

MESSAGE SENT: Wednesday, December 9, 2009, 00:36.
SUBJECT: just got back from TeguciGOLPE

Hi Andrés, how's it going? Here everything's terrible and there's no end to the bad news. I just got back from TeguciGOLPE, Honduras, after two months doing interviews with poets (Roberto Sosa, Rigoberto Paredes, José Adán Castelar), activists, and Artists in Resistance, and advisers and intermediaries of President Zelaya (I did a minireport with him, by phone, because they didn't allow me to enter the Brazilian embassy). Things are unstable in Honduras. A certain Billy Joya (a Honduran trained by the Argentine secret military police and the military guards in Chile under Pinochet) is one of Micheletti's ministers, and the de facto regime is a kind of replay of the Dirty War. I fell in love with Tegucigalpa, I was almost deported in a military operation. . . . Man, what a trip.

*

Over the rooms and windows shadowed by abandonment.
Over the flight of spring, drowned yesterday
in a glass of water.
Over the old melancholia (woven
and unwoven slowly), daughter
of the great betrayals of our parents and our grandparents:
we're alone.

—ROBERTO SOSA

I, on the other hand, don't harbor anything: neither hope nor anger.
One by one they gave me the glories I deserved
and I was defeated with their best weapons.
Love is the only battle
that is fought on equal terms.

—RIGOBERTO PAREDES

. . . and here, almost at my feet, the water runs
aimlessly toward the sea.

—JOSÉ ADÁN CASTELAR

14

Miami, Beyond the Palm Trees

GUATEMALA AIRPORT. Preboarding zone. American Airlines counter. When the agent sees that I have carry-on luggage, she anxiously asks me if I have liquids (yes, I do), what they are (gel, shampoo, cologne), how many ounces they contain (how much exactly is an ounce?), if I have Ziploc bags (excuse me?), if something's wrong with me or if I'm stupid (yes, I am), if I'm sure that I don't want to check my bag (no, I don't). The agent looks at me as I imagine one looks at a novice hang glider, hands me my boarding pass, and takes a deep breath.

*

Boarding area. International terminal. Security check. Jacket. Watch. Keys. Belt. Coins. Computer. Chargers. Cords. Pullover. Nail clippers. Razor. Lotion. Shoes. My liver and pancreas do not need to be taken out.

*

Miami seems irreversibly ugly, until one lands at night among its lights.

*

"You have not filled out the green form." The bilingual policeman speaks to me in English. No, sir, I respond. "You filled out the white

179

one." Yes, sir, I respond. "Go fill out the green one and come back." Yes, sir. "On my computer I see you did not complete the preflight procedure." No, sir. "You should have done it." Yes, sir. "Technically, we shouldn't let you in. That's the law." Yes, sir. "Next time, do it." Yes sir. "Otherwise . . . " Yes, sir. Yes, sir. Yes, sir. Welcome. Welcome. Welcome.

*

HOTEL IN MIAMI: Hyatt Regency.
HOTEL ENVIRONMENT: Shopping Mall with Beds.
RECEPTION STYLE: *Extremely Kind*, Señor.

*

On South Miami Avenue, where there used to be an old fire station, they've opened an irresistible Spanish restaurant. Irresistible not because of its food, but because of its extraordinary name: Dolores But You Can Call Me Lolita. They created an intertextual restaurant. We dine on the terrace. We eat croquettes. The well-built waiter says his name is Margaret.

*

People don't walk here either, but for different reasons. In many Latin American cities, walking is unsafe. In Miami, it's unproductive.

*

"This," someone says, "is a writers' city." Why? I ask, perplexed. "Just listen—Mi-a-mí, me-to-me, just like all the writers!"

*

A widespread, throbbing sensuality. A chromatic elasticity in the skin. A trace of the gym in every navel. Cars, sandals, money.

*

Noon. Ocean Drive. The raucous heart of Miami Beach. Convertibles. Palm trees. The fascination of kitsch as a way of life. By the door of Mango's, a Latin dance bar, a group of half-black dancers, dressed in leotards, move their hips distractedly. Right now the place is almost empty. A lone couple, maybe survivors from the night before, twirl around the dance floor. Meanwhile, Miami twirls around itself.

*

Miami Beach's mythology disappoints me, but its sociology surprises me. Its beaches and boulevards aren't so great. Its Latin synthesis, on the other hand, its mix of placeless Spanish, its tan and swaying Hispanic Frankenstein, is like a foreshadowing of the future.

*

Moving through Coral Gables, I can't help but recall Juan Ramón Jiménez. This city was the first of his dignified exile, just after the end of the Spanish Civil War. Here he wrote *Romances de Coral Gables*. These verses sprang from here: "I don't want to return to myself / for fear of provoking the distaste of a different tree / among so many identical trees / The trees forgot my condition of wandering man / and, with my condition forgotten, / I heard the trees speak . . . / How could I tell them / that I was just a passerby, / that they shouldn't speak to me? / I didn't want to betray them. / He never betrayed the people of Spain or the trees of Miami."

*

In Coconut Grove there are Jamaicans, Bahamians, and white people. Suddenly, beyond a certain street, the latter group disappears from the map. In the same neighborhood, we're now in the black area. The white people don't seem to pass through it and the black people don't leave it. A tacit game of checkers. With a board divided in two.

*

I visit Little Havana, with plenty of home-cooked meals, small shops, and signs in Spanish. Among the souvenirs, one gift catches my eye: rolls of toilet paper with the bearded likeness of Fidel. This would be unthinkable in Cuba. Not because of censorship, but because of the lack of toilet paper.

*

"There are people who have lived here for twenty years," she says, "and still don't dare to say Fidel's name. They call him the Unnameable One."

*

Versailles Restaurant is a popular bastion of Cuban dissidents. Here they make wonderful food and hand out anti-Castro publications. I sit down to read and order a *cortadito*. "Three European countries," I read in *Spotlight*, "ask Spain to clarify its position toward Cuba. The next European presidency is a concern for some members, particularly with respect to future foreign relations." At the next table I hear complaints about the Spanish government for its silence regarding the detention of blogger Yoani Sánchez, who received a beating as a calculated warning. When it rains, it pours. I don't remember any big official protests last year when they refused to give her permission to travel to Spain to receive a prize for her exemplary work as a reporter.

*

The paper *Art Deco Tropical* attempts a strange defense of Yoani Sánchez: "Weak like a woman, but also strong . . . " There should be a denunciation of such denunciations.

*

In *La píldora del mal amor* by Anjanette Delgado, a light novel about heavy pains, the protagonist answers her husband, "You say you love me because you don't know me very well."

*

The controversial awarding of the Nobel Peace Prize to Obama has caused a commotion in the Cuban papers in Miami, particularly those on the Republican far right. I read an article by Saturnino Polón, who had the undeniably bad fortune of being a political prisoner of Castro, in *Enfoque 3*. The author constantly refers to Obama by his middle name, Hussein, as if this coincidental overlap with the Iraqi dictator might lead to intelligent conclusions. Although Mr. Polón calls himself a writer, I'll allow myself to touch up his punctuation to make the text more legible: "The awarding of the prize, years ago, to the lying Rigoberta Menchú, heralded our current moment. But the final proof that this prize is merely an instrument of manipulation was given to us by the impudent decision to award the prize to B. Hussein Obama. . . . Mr. Hussein has not yet done anything for peace, apart from being a complete charlatan. . . . That's why this opportunistic charlatan whom we must by law call the president was hired, when we don't even know if he's actually president, since he has never shown his birth certificate. . . . Additionally, having been raised with and spoon-fed fundamentalist Muslim ideas, radical pro-Communist leftist ideas, and racist and radical leftist ideas from the Black Power movement. . . . Now he's under even more pressure than before to achieve some *peace* at all costs. Of course, the most obvious way would be to stop the current war (it would be better to call it a 'campaign') in Muslim Asia. . . . The conclusion is simple. Nothing has contributed more to the cause of World Peace, nor helped to prevent the repetition of large-scale wars like World War I and World War II nor made these current wars manageable than the very existence of nuclear arms. . . . Nobody has more right to the prize than the Atomic Bomb. That has been the most effective promoter of World Peace among men." I breathe deeply. This article would have particular success in Hiroshima and Nagasaki. I have the feeling that I've just been witness to an extraordinary lesson, but I'm not exactly sure about what.

*

More reasonably, two readers in the pages of the same newspaper synthesize the matter succinctly: "Unfortunately, the president's popularity has overshadowed those who have been struggling tirelessly all of their lives to truly achieve peace and human rights." "Leaders at the helm of powerful nations with significant weight in world events should be exempt from receiving the Nobel Peace Prize. At least while they're representing their country. . . . Conflicts of interest necessarily exist." *Spotlight* formulates this into a good question: "Is it possible that the charismatic Barack Obama . . . has adopted Henry Kissinger's model of political realism to shape the country's foreign affairs, a model that exudes pragmatism but that lacks any passion for freedom and human rights?" It then mentions relations with China, Egypt, Russia, and, of course, Cuba. *Passion for freedom and human rights.* Maybe these values are incompatible with passion itself.

*

"There is a segment of the Cuban dissidence," she says, "that maintains, in my view, a profound complicity with the regime over there. They do them so many favors!"

*

"But in Cuba," someone objects, "at least there has always been education and health care." "Ay, *mi hermano*," someone else answers, "but nobody spends their whole life in a hospital or in school!" "Yeah," a third adds, "there they teach everyone to read. To read the Party line."

*

In Miami the sun illuminates, penetrates, castrates you. It's a Castro-like heat.

*

"Tomás Regalado is the typical politician defending big interests," someone argues. "Which in Miami," someone else points out, "is completely redundant."

*

"May God keep her where it's not wet," she says seriously, referring to a dead woman.

*

I stop to eat at Exquisito, a restaurant in Little Havana where they welcome smokers at the entrance. The place is covered with tiles and old pictures of Cuban musicians: Arturo Sandoval, Roberto Torres, Concha Valdés Miranda. In one of the corners there is a stash of percussion instruments used in their shows. I ask for a papaya shake and fried rice. I'm curious to see if it's similar to what in Spain they call *arroz a la cubana*. I ask the waitress how they cook it. "Just like in China," she answers.

*

I take a walk through Little Haiti, a poor, desolate, and fascinating neighborhood that has nothing to do with the Miami we see on TV. Here they speak Creole, a language that appears on most of the signs. On 54th Street I see a Haitian Baptist church, a Halouba voodoo temple, and a Philadelphia Church of God, with the slogan "*Église de Dieu de Philadelphie, Inc. Prepare-toi à la Rencontre de ton Dieu!*" If only the Catholic Church were as clear in its intentions.

*

The Halouba temple is actually a store that sells religious articles and books. It's filled with dolls and sculptures. They speak English and Spanish. They offer treatment for any problem. Out of respect, they prohibit parking in front of the door. They accept Visa, MasterCard, and American Express.

*

I go into a bar named Chez le Bebe. I order a grapefruit juice. I hear people switching from Creole (among themselves) to English (among strangers). A sign says, "No Ticket No Food!! No Tike No Manje!! No Excuse No Pardon!!" They all look at me, look at my notebook. I pay for my juice and leave. A hoarse preacher passes by the door shouting about the end of the world with a speaker on his shoulder.

*

Conceptually speaking, sickness and contagion do not exist in Haitian culture. This, it goes without saying, multiplies their effects. All suffering results from the evil eye, the struggle of ritual, foreign curses. Regarding foreign curses, one tends to agree.

*

There are at least three greetings in Creole. In French, "Bonjour." Colloquially, "Sak Pasé" ("What's up?"). And traditionally: "One! Respe!" ("Honor! Respect!"). The last greeting comes from the countryside and seems like less of a greeting than a historical demand. One that has never been fulfilled.

*

Miami, melting pot or collection of ghettos? To be honest, here the mixture of cultures only occurs among people of a single color: dollar-green.

*

On Saturday morning I take my dirty clothes to the hotel laundry. But apparently the Gringo Union of Active Laundry Workers of

African-American Ethnicity, or something like that, has struck down the possibility of offering services on the weekend. I know this because the receptionist at one of the biggest hotels in the entire city tells me that any article of clothing received after eight a.m. on Saturday won't be returned until Monday. Since my plane leaves on Sunday and the underwear I have on is my last clean pair, the next morning I get up early to buy some more. After various traffic jams I get out on busy Lincoln Road, which I walk down quickly, wearing yesterday's underwear. After much searching, I find underwear that's not multicolored and doesn't sport the image of a superhero. I arrive late for a meeting, have lunch without taking a break, and head immediately to the airport. There I try to change my clothes, but when I open up the box I discover that the salesperson forgot to take off the plastic security tag. So not only can I not put them on, but I also won't be able to pass through security without alarms ringing everywhere. The mere thought of explaining to a US guard armed with a pistol that this pair of Calvin Klein underwear, the only clean pair I have, is not stolen and doesn't contain explosives, is enough to send shivers down my spine. So I put the underwear back in the box, find a trashcan, throw away twenty-two dollars of cotton and polyester, accept my uncleanliness, and begin to feel almost innocent.

15

San Juan, Complementary and Under Construction

"WHEN YOU GET TO PUERTO RICO," a Puerto Rican friend tells me in Miami, "although you'll see the gringo lifestyle everywhere and the three common American principles of passports, dollars, and defense, when you actually talk to people, you'll think the same thing as everyone else who goes there: 'Shit, this is Latin America!'"

*

"The sky has fallen," they announce when I arrive.

*

HOTEL IN SAN JUAN: Condado Plaza.
HOTEL ENVIRONMENT: Casino with a View.
RECEPTION STYLE: Not Exactly Gringo.

*

Puerto Rican bilingualism sometimes works like Google Translate, copying words and syntactic structures from English. When I arrive, they announce that the airport is "under construction"—"*bajo construcción*" rather than "*en obras.*" In the hotel, they explain to me that Wi-Fi is "complimentary"—"*complementario*" rather than "*gratuito.*" A friend tells me that if I need anything, I should literally "*let* him know"—"*déjamelo saber,*" not "*me dices*" or "*me avisas.*" The

Spanish they speak here is simultaneously familiar and strange, under construction, the English elements complementary. If the language needs something, it takes it. And it no longer knows where it's coming from.

*

I eat breakfast by a window facing the rebellious waves of the Atlantic. But I don't hear the waves. I hear neutral music and the occasional grunts of the hotel casino, where compulsive early-morning gamblers are also sitting down to breakfast. This is Puerto Rico: the sea on one side, the American roulette wheel on the other.

*

Last night there was a storm. The city awakens to physical damage and traffic jams. The caravan of cars moves slowly past a sign for tourists on Highway 2: "Smile, Puerto Rico! Everything is fresh today."

*

There are three main political parties. The blue party, or Nuevo Progresista, which advocates for incorporation into the United States. The red party, or Popular Democrático, which defends the island's current status as a free associated state. And the green party, or Independentista Puertorriqueño, which tends to act from its minority position as the arbiter between the other two. The *independentistas* led the civil protests in Vieques, the small island where the American armed forces did military exercises until it was shown that they caused environmental damage and posed major health risks. The flip side of Yankee privilege. I ask a friend who votes for the blue party, which is now in power, why not become independent? "It scares us," he responds sensibly, "because we would end up in the hands of the rich people here." So I ask him why not remain as they are. Why become part of the United States? "Well, because, well, I don't kn . . . " my friend answers, beginning his reply in English before switching back to Spanish. "To get ahead of the curve, you know, to be more prepared when they force us to choose between staying or leaving. Yeah, that's it. Politics isn't my strong suit."

*

I stop for coffee at La Viña, a bakery run by a family of Spanish descent. The place is full, though one high chair remains empty with the following warning: "Seat reserved for M. Abraham." A little while later an old bald man enters, dressed in Bermuda shorts, with a string of lottery tickets around his neck. He sits there and starts looking at us with a lost gaze, without making any apparent move to sell anything to anyone.

*

Channel 6, Puerto Rico TV. "Now that everyone is saying 'No to the war, no to the war,'" declares an actor, "I would ask for a little pity." If pity existed, they wouldn't torment the audience by interviewing the first person with a spare moment.

*

"Recording this album," says the former lead singer of the group Sin Bandera, "was like being on the Barcelona soccer team: whoever comes, whoever plays, it sounds great." In Puerto Rico soccer barely exists. There isn't even a professional league. Messi is Pan-Hispanic.

*

The bay of San Juan has a melancholic beauty. It flows gently into the Atlantic, like someone falling asleep right before drowning.

*

In the Plaza Cristóbal Colón we find the Pablo Casals Museum, the great Catalan cellist who married a Puerto Rican woman near the end of his life, returned to his mother's homeland, and ended up being adopted as the illustrious child and musical father of the island. Columbus discovered a land to invade. Casals invaded it with discoveries.

*

Old San Juan, the exquisite historic district in the capital, has a variety of cobblestone streets, colorful facades, and hip shops. Most people are tourists ("Welcome-*Willkommen-Bienvenue*"), wealthy ("Jewelry repairs while you wait"), or artists (galleries and art stores abound). A young homeless man walks by, and into these notes of mine, and starts digging through a trash bin.

*

Just below the historic district, behind a large wall, is La Perla. Ironically, "The Pearl" is a poor neighborhood, with tin houses and a certain reputation for crime, drugs, and shootouts that some of my friends confirm and others deny. The two parts of the city's downtown (and perhaps two groups of friends) are separated by a wall, by history, by the police.

*

I read a story by Yolanda Arroyo Pizarro: "I tried to get close to her, but the masses prevented me. Also, someone who was closer than I was to the fence, with a sign that read 'Drug- and Weapon-Free Zone,' had already tried my idea and got in the middle . . . only to receive a large dose of rebel punches."

*

Different accent, different bodies. An accent with curves. Overflowing and self-fulfilling legs and butts, flaunting the independence that this island will never have.

*

Always, everywhere, Juan Ramón Jiménez. Also in Puerto Rico. The poet arrived in San Juan after a long exile. The life he made for himself here gave rise to, among other things, the volume *Isla de la simpatía*, recently reissued by the University of Puerto Rico's publishing house. It's revealing to read a Juan Ramón who is radically progressive in questions of language: non-Eurocentric and ahead of his time—and not just for the Spain that he lived in (and had to abandon). "I believe in the ceaseless evolution of language," he writes, "and especially of the Spanish language or languages. I believe, like Unamuno, that Hispanism means nothing if not the universality of Spanish— that is, an acceptance of the many different ways of speaking Spanish." In other words, a web of archipelagos connected by the same sea of language. In another passage, I read, "A poem is an island."

*

"Tea, tea?" she responds, widening her eyes. "Oh God, I don't know. Coffee yes, wherever you go. But tea!" And she offers me my seventh coffee of the day.

*

Suddenly all of my literary ghosts, my ghosts from both sides of the Atlantic, sally forth during my visit to the Río Piedras campus of the University of Puerto Rico. I receive an anniversary edition of Cortázar's legendary translation of Poe, commissioned more than fifty years ago by the Granada-born Francisco Ayala. This edition includes engravings by the artist Nelson Sambolín. I flip through the volume I know least, the one that contains Poe's essays and criticism. I find ideas that seem to have been formulated not a hundred and fifty years ago but a month and a half ago. "They tell us that the most precise way to calculate the value of a work is to find out how many readers it has. The question 'Does the book sell?' entails for them everything you need to say or state about quality in the book market." I wonder if the Romantic era was really that romantic.

*

"A translation," I read in the prologue to the new edition of Poe, "must remain at the same time close to and distant from its object in order to recreate it in another language." It occurs to me that the same process would be desirable for any work written in one's mother tongue. To remain close and far away from the language to create it anew. A serendipitous corner, this bilingual island of Puerto Rico, for thinking about our everyday mechanics of translation.

*

Mayra Santos-Febres's writing is a miraculous mixture of reflection and rage. From *Sirena Selena* to the recent *Fe en disfraz*, her novels view sex as a semantic field and masks as various layers of skin. If every body is a book, as the poet would have it, this book denudes its darkest chapters. Eroticizing conflicts, problematizing eroticism. "To always be moving among various worlds," explains Santos-Febres, whose essays take the form of a vast cartography, "has marked and enriched us. As Puerto Ricans, we robbed a passport and learned to live with a false (or better yet an interposed) identity. . . . The divorce law took effect in Puerto Rico in 1901. That meant that many women supported the North American invasion, because for them it signaled freedom from many of the patriarchal controls instituted by the *criollo* society. . . . This is a country where translation and mobility are part of daily life. . . . You must learn to navigate several linguistic, cultural, historical, and even legal codes at the same time. . . . They are streets, paths, and routes that are always changing places. . . . A map on top of a map on top of a map."

*

We order the light local beer, Medalla. I must admit we receive our award many times over.

*

And after the winds, finally, there's sun. Or rather, the sun proposes a finale: this moment of fullness, blue and green, when the waves fold time, suggesting I stay longer. I make a promise and turn back from the hotel's lookout point. "Warning: wet floor," I read as I walk.

*

Planes incessantly pass over the hotel, going to or coming from the nearby airport, uniting land with land. If there's a place in the world where one understands how living surrounded by the sea isolates and communicates, encloses and gives perspective, brings things closer and moves them farther away, that place is Puerto Rico.

*

I read through recent works by local authors, the shortest line between curiosity and knowledge about a place. In *Reyerta TV*, Juan Luis Ramos's first book of short stories, I read, "I became a rat, an octopus, a hound of modernity." That could be the autobiography of all young Latin American writers. In *Intemperie*, Nicole Cecilia Delgado's poetry volume, I find, "Returning, I retain: yearning for the outdoors / a different notion of time . . . a different notion of water . . . / a different notion about silence and pathways." That could be the autobiography of all travelers.

*

In Plaza Ballajá there is a totem pole made from fragments of various pre-Columbian ceramics. The idea, I suppose, is to symbolically reconstruct the ruined cultures, propping them up against colonial aggressions. I look closely at the totem pole and notice there are several parts that are damaged. I ask what happened. They tell me that a French tourist, drunk out of his mind, climbed up the monument and broke various pieces. Colonialism is neither created nor destroyed, only transformed. Or inebriated.

*

In San Juan it's hot a priori. Even when it rains and cools off, people assume that it's boiling outside, put their air conditioning on high, and use tons of ice. When you tell them it's cold outside, they look puzzled, then say that you're right and offer you an ice-cold beer.

*

I hang out with a group of university students. *Janguear*, they say, borrowing the English verb. We go to Río Piedras, the student city within the city. We drink in a bar named Boricua, a popular spot with live jazz. The vibe is great but a bit too low-key, like a cautious party. Later I find out that about three months ago, police raided a few buildings over on Avenida Universidad. They used tear gas and some students were injured. "This government," says one student, "is the worst in history. Their policy is to make everything illegal. They act like we're in the Cold War. They repress student movements, without realizing that we move precisely because of their repression."

*

San Juan airport. Security. While I wait in line, I wonder what will happen to me; leaving the United States tends to be as bad as entering. I go through the standard inspection control: take out my computer, take off my clothes, put on my nice face, etc. Suddenly I'm routed toward a policeman who repeatedly shouts, "Passports! Tickets! IDs! Passports! Tickets! IDs!" He looks at my boarding pass and says "Andrés." I continue. Right after, I hear at my back "Jorge" and "María." Then the policeman turns to his friend and tells him "They're all *folks*," or something like that. His friend nods, and they separate us from the line and begin to search us more thoroughly.

16

Santo Domingo, the Cardinal in the Tunnel

I'M SURPRISED, WHEN I LAND, to see quotes from Columbus's diaries reproduced on the walls. Columbus called this island Hispaniola. In the airport they seem to celebrate that. I take out my Spanish passport with some relief.

*

Again: first last name, second last name, married name. When gay marriage and sex changes become legal worldwide, some countries' customs forms will get very complicated.

*

At night, on the way to the hotel, I'm struck by an infinite row of streetlights, none of which are lit. "Welcome to darkness," says my hostess.

*

We pass several motels, referred to here with the bucolic or deceptive name "cabins." One of them is called Villa España. Unlike the others, this island definitely copulates with the Motherland.

*

I share my first impression with a friend. Isn't there a less combative relationship with the colonial past in the Dominican Republic? "Maybe," he answers. "Not a single native was left here." The dictator Trujillo was in charge of the latter stages of the evangelization process, which included a concordat with the Vatican. Today Cardinal López Rodríguez has introduced an antiabortion clause into the national constitution. As I mentioned, there isn't a single native left.

*

Can we think of Trujillo without thinking of Vargas Llosa's *The Feast of the Goat*? In the long run, fiction assails institutions more effectively than armies.

*

HOTEL IN SANTO DOMINGO: Sol Meliá.
HOTEL ENVIRONMENT: Motherland with Interior Palm Trees.
RECEPTION STYLE: Slllloooowwww, Sir.

*

"When you go to the Dominican Republic," some Puerto Rican friends predicted, "they will lavish you in ceremony." When I get to the hotel, the reception concierge calls a butler. The butler shows me to a higher floor, where I am helped at a second, more private reception desk. The concierge at the second reception desk gives me a hotel welcome letter, signed by the manager of Royal Service. On the list of services mentioned in the letter, the last two are "light press of four articles of clothing" and "shoe shine on the day of arrival."

*

An invitation, in an envelope, for the "First Spanish Cooking Festival, November 17–30. Restaurante Da Vinci. Chefs invited from L'Albufera restaurant in Seville." *Joder*.

*

Dominican manners revolve around the intangible. People seem to move as if gliding across a recently waxed floor. They speak in a low cadence, prudently. They look at you lightly, without challenging you. They pick up objects gently, as if trying not to break or stain them. I'm not sure whether this is courtesy or residual fear.

*

We order the local beer, Presidente, "Pride of the Dominicans." I ask if this has anything to do ... "Yes, yes," they explain, "that's why, he's why." Now I understand its singularly bitter taste.

*

In *Listín Diario*, the oldest newspaper in the country, I read, "According to a historian, Columbus was a spy. Manuel Rosa's book *Colón: La historia nunca contada*, maintains that the admiral misled Ferdinand of Aragon and Isabella of Castile into opening a new route toward the false Indies, in order to give the Portuguese an unimpeded path to the real Indies." Columbus as a double agent. Latin America as the secondary effect of a conspiracy. The expansion of the Spanish language as the unpredictable profit of betrayal. Borges would have loved it.

*

Junot Díaz was born in Santo Domingo, went to school in New Jersey, and teaches in Massachusetts. He learned to speak in Spanish and to write in English, and he won a Pulitzer. His first book, *Los boys*, the original English title of which is *Drown*, narrates with painful humor the racism and classism within US minority communities. The othering within otherness itself. "Order everything in your busted-up Spanish," recommends the short story, "How to Date a Brown Girl (Black Girl, White Girl, or Halfie)." "Let her correct you if she's Latina and amaze her if she's black. . . . A halfie will tell you that her parents met in the Movement. . . . Put down your hamburger and say, It must have been hard. She will appreciate your interest. She will tell you more. Black people, she will say, treat me real bad. That's why I don't like them. You'll wonder how she feels about Dominicans. Don't ask. . . . She'll say, I like Spanish guys, and even though you've never been to Spain, say, I like you. You'll sound smooth."

*

On the lovely Calle Las Damas—that is, The Ladies—you'll find the gentlemen. That is, the National Pantheon. General Pedro Santana, for example, an ambiguous and conservative liberator, who fought to separate the island from the Haitians and reannex it to the Spanish Crown. General Gregorio Luperón, who also has a niche, was mixed race and worked to undo Santana's work. In the pantheon there are poets (Gastón Fernando Deligne), historians (José Gabriel García), and pessimistic intellectuals (Américo Lugo). There don't seem to be women except for Concepción Bona, who stitched the first national flag. I am surprised to see flat niches with still-nameless plaques. I ask why. "We don't have enough heroes," my guide answers.

*

Osiris Vallejo's poetry volume *Saint Domingue, 2044* invokes the complex relationship between Dominican identity and Haiti. The contributions, the forgetting, the violence. The interesting thing is that he does it by looking not only at the past but also at the future: a sort of prophecy of the present. This doubling of time alludes to a second person, the sender and addressee of the verses. In one of the poems, I read, "On the nameless afternoon in which we are not that / which we wished for in eighteen hundred . . . / But you don't know that." And, later in the book, and in time, "You no longer drown in the sea as you used to, but now in the midst of enemy territory / that you used to call an island of your own / even though it was one of two halves."

*

I enter the stunning Catedral de Santa María la Menor, the first cathedral in the Americas. Cardinal López Rodríguez, the antiabortion crusader, lives just behind it, in a colonial mansion. They say there's a tunnel that connects his room with the cathedral, so that His Excellency need not cross the street. More exactly: the tunnel or catacomb reaches all the way to the Vatican.

*

Here surgery seems like less of an option than a starting point. I look at the store windows, the bursting clothes, the silicone-filled manikins.

*

Militant graffiti on the corner of Calle Arzobispo Meriño: "That's not my constitution!" Women could write the exact same thing beside the manikins in the store windows.

*

Aída Cartagena Portalatín was perhaps the most important Dominican woman writer of the twentieth century. She was an essayist and art critic. Her novel *Escalera para Electra* was close to winning the Biblioteca Breve Prize, but got tripped up on the last rung of the ladder, the same one that entangled the feet of so many women of the time. More than anything else, she was a poet. In her poetry volume *Una mujer está sola*, I read, "A woman is alone. Alone with her stature. / With her eyes open. With her arms open. . . . / Nobody comes forward to offer her a suit / to dress up her voice."

*

"You say Christ suffered, and received ten lashes, and was happy?" reasons a drunkard. "Girl, forget about that! The guy died forever ago, get yourself another rum."

*

"Vandalism," *Listín Diario* laments on its cover. "Several unidentified persons painted the columns of the main entrance to the cathedral with the phrase 'That's not my constitution,' the slogan used by some minority groups that are against the new Magna Carta." Thanks to the cover, they are now a little less of a minority.

*

I read *Palomos*, by the novelist and hip-hop expert Pedro Antonio Valdez, which recounts the lives of youth gangs to the beat of rap and reggaeton. The novel includes an index of songs that, to the credit of the author, introduces an imagined soundtrack, doing away with any device that might not hold up to time. In one of the chapters, a high-school principal puts together a competition for patriotic poetry. She brings all the students together outside. She makes them say the Lord's Prayer. Then she launches into "a speech about the right way to speak" while, the narrator observes, "the son-of-a-bitch sun roasts their brains." In an involuntary display of her knowledge of Dominican slang, the principal proclaims, "A student of this school will never use the word '*jeva*,' to refer to a girl, or '*palomo*' for a freshman, or '*quillar*,' for hassling. He will never say '*janguear*,' for spending time with someone, or '*bufear*,' for making fun, or '*tripear*,' for joking . . ." At the same time a wayward student recites, "Never say 'fornicate,' but '*singar*' . . . Never say 'penis,' but '*güebo*' . . . Never say 'vagina,' but '*toto*' . . . "

*

I read the Spanish press to stay connected to Spain—if, that is, digital news is actually located somewhere. ABC publishes an obituary for Jeanne-Claude, the wife and collaborator of the land artist Christo, "famous for wrapping, along with her husband . . . the Reichstag in Berlin and the Pont Neuf in Paris, as well as for filling Central Park with seven thousand gates." Filling everything with gates: that's what art and the Internet do. In *El País* I find an interview with the photographer Alex Webb, who declares, "There is a third country between the United States and Mexico: the border." Maybe there, on The Border, is where all passports should be processed.

*

Smoking is prohibited in enclosed areas. All except for one, O inveterate Hispanism: Centro Asturiano de Santo Domingo, where patrons happily puff away.

*

This sticky, exhausting heat, which in the long run wears down your hope.

*

"I prefer," she says, "not to read Dominican works. I don't like seeing myself reflected in books; I want to read about other places, other places."

*

Yesterday, in downtown La Habana, supporters of the Castro regime attacked blogger Yoani Sánchez's husband. There is video and photographic evidence of the incident. Of course, not everyone releases the same information. The Argentine news outlet *La Nación* quotes a disturbing announcement from the Cuban government: "Security agents, whom Yoani Sánchez has repeatedly accused of assault and harassment, removed her husband from the scene so that he would not suffer the anger of a people tired of so many provocations." The Castro regime prides itself on taking measures that are basic to the function of any government: celebrating an unbiased trial, authorizing a concert, or preventing the public lynching of an opposition figure. The official report seems not to view physical aggression against a citizen as a punishable offense. Rather, it shows compassion for the attackers, who had been *provoked* ideologically. In his personal blog, which doesn't attract as much attention as his wife's, Escobar gives thanks for his "double fortune" of having friends who defended him and "a foreign press that filmed everything." It shouldn't be necessary to mention the media presence as a fortunate coincidence: Escobar has every right in the world to alert them and take precautions for his own safety. On the Catalan site *Kaosenlared*, the facts take on a different cast. The headline copies the government report: "People are tired of Yoani Sánchez. A group of youths silenced the blogger's husband with the rhythms of the conga and shouts in favor of the revolution." Below there is a picture of attractive and peaceful young men. "Youth to the front," reads the photo's caption. On the same site, Salim Lamrani, a professor at the Sorbonne, questions the authenticity of a previous attack on the blogger that was not caught on camera. Lamrani criticizes the dissemination of the news in "the Western media," implying that Cuba is outside of the West, and considers it "illogical that the Cuban authorities would publically mistreat such a high-profile dissident" because, he argues, "there are more effective and discreet measures for intimidating the opposition." Are there, Professor? We assumed as much.

*

Pedro Henríquez Ureña was the greatest Dominican humanist. Like Martí, he dreamed of the Americas as a single land. "No revolution," I read in *Ideario*, an incredible collection of his thoughts, "fails to receive the inheritance of the regime that has fallen."

*

Tomorrow there will be a demonstration against gender violence along the Santo Domingo boardwalk. Meanwhile, *Listín Diario* reports, "The first lady initiates an act to condemn violence against women. In the meeting held last night at the National Palace, Monsignor Arnaiz expressed the need for forgiveness." Any abuser would agree: though she might occasionally deserve a beating, all wives should be forgiven. Or was Monsignor speaking of forgiving the abusers? Theology is complex. I continue reading. "Monsignor Francisco José Arnaiz . . . said that domestic violence is a cultural problem deeply rooted in the Dominican population, a historical phenomenon that can only be countered spiritually." Very unspiritually, I wonder if it would help for women to have more rights, jobs, and money of their own. "Each participant," the article continues, "presented a ten-minute reflection emphasizing the need for society to organize its conduct so that women are thought of as mothers and wives who help their men in their moments of greatest need." On this basis, the abuser reasons as he leaves Mass, if his wife decides to leave him, beating her is almost a question of principles. Amen.

*

"Nothing is less pure than the barbarian," Henríquez Ureña warns. "His moral life is a perpetual struggle between his fear of his own instincts and his desire to justify them."

*

In Plaza de España, a dance company organizes a show of popular dance. They are accompanied by an orchestra with an accordion. They dance the criollo waltz, the *carabiné* ("*a bailar el carabiné, / a bailarlo en la punta' el pie. / Cara sucia, compra jabón / pa' que laves tu camisón*"), Dominican merengues, and tap dances that bring to mind flamenco. We are surrounded by music, soft-drink vendors, food stands. Kids dance, skate, and play with balls. Below everything is joyful and carefree. Above, the tense sky announces a storm.

*

At the end of the plaza, in the Palacio Virreinal that housed Diego Colón, the long-deceased governor of Santo Domingo and son of the Admiral, we see an exhibit that recreates early palace life. The actors try to imitate Renaissance speech and the Castilian accent, comically putting z's wherever they can: *zeñor, tezoro, situazión, vozotros*, etc. Through the windows of the palace, from the Plaza de España, come the thumping rhythms of a bachata.

*

"They're so ungrateful it makes little sense to treat them well," the master concludes in Juan Bosch's Quirogaesque short story "Los amos." Besides being a splendid short-story writer and essayist, Juan Bosch was the first democratic president after Trujillo's assassination. His Partido Revolucionario Dominicano won the elections, a world-shattering event in the country. A few months later, the masters of the army overthrew him for being ungrateful: you give the people democracy and they repay you by wanting reform. Today Bosch's party is in power. And of course they support the criminalization of abortion.

*

I read in *Eva/Sión/Es*, a book by the poet and playwright Chiqui Vicioso, "Upright I give birth to myself / and my water breaks / in a wave of curses / and challenges."

*

La Cafetera is almost invisible, maybe because it forms part of the urban landscape. Just as we scarcely pay attention to the ripples on the surface of water, the tremble of leaves, or the profiles of the hills, the oldest café in the city goes unnoticed. Hidden in the midst of the pedestrian street El Conde, its entrance is smooth, white, and virtually a discouragement to entering. According to Edu, one of the managers, they serve "the best coffee in the world, from Russia to Tierra del Fuego." In La Cafetera one can rest, debate, play chess (games in which the winner is determined by who has the quickest jokes, not who puts whom in checkmate), and reminisce. A plaque presides over the entrance: "To the Spanish intellectuals and artists exiled in 1939 and the Dominicans who took them in." Toward the back, the roof is slanted. Any member of the coffee dynasty may take your order; the waiters form a family that regular customers eventually join. Like a coffee blend, La Cafetera mixes together artists, neighbors, celebrities, and ordinary people. Suddenly Beti passes by the door. "What are you doing here?" they ask her. "Nothing," she answers, "just stretching out my little feet."

*

On the way to the airport, driving along Avenida España, traffic suddenly comes to a halt. A long line of vehicles passes at five miles an hour. "It must be a funeral," says the driver. "Here, you can't hurry the dead." When the avenue forks, we drive past a long black car and accelerate.

*

The ideal for all music lovers, writes Henríquez Ureña, would be to maintain at the same time "an always-virginal perception" and a "memory rich in wisdom.". The same thing could be said of the traveler.

17

Panama, Permanently Temporary

AS SOON AS I LAND, I notice that the Panama airport doesn't look like any other airport in the region. It is much broader, busier, and better equipped. Its daily traffic, according to a strangely precise airport employee, is 160 flights. As if the fate of this small country were to connect the world.

*

While waiting in the immigration line, I'm struck by another difference: the first ads the traveler sees are not for government, tourism, or telecommunications. The first offering, at seven-figure prices, is resort homes.

*

"We are," he tells me, "Indocentralamericangringos. When you go to the mall, you'll think, 'What gringos!' When you visit the schools, you'll think, 'What Indians!'"

*

On the way to the hotel, I'm surprised by the crowded profile of skyscrapers. The effect is a mix of Miami and real-estate speculation. I'm told, with the same strange precision, as if in Panama such statistics were more important than in other places, that the financial area has over 150 banks (almost as many banks as flights, I think) and that Donald Trump does big business here. I crack a smile when they tell me that this part of the city is often referred to as Marbella, like the Andalusian city. On one side of the highway, beneath the formidable buildings, I make out a quiet, shady zone at ground level. I ask about it and they tell me it's the fishing village Boca La Caja.

*

HOTEL IN PANAMA: Bristol.
HOTEL ENVIRONMENT: Super Executive.
RECEPTION STYLE: Asian Entourage.

*

My room has fruit, cable, and wireless Internet, a fax machine, a crystal shower with separate bath, a dozen towels, gilded bathroom fittings, a king-size bed, a DVD player, a radio, an alarm clock with iPod speakers, a suit brush, an umbrella, a cold-drink kit, and antique lamps. I look at the window. Boca La Caja is nowhere in sight.

*

Before, the city was divided in two: half for the Panamanians, half for the Americans. A wall and a fence spanned the street that at that time was called Avenida 4 de Julio. Fifty years ago, a group of students crossed it to place the Panama flag on the US side alongside the American flag, as the current treaty allows. The police fired on the students and killed several of them. Today that avenue, along which our car is driving, is called Avenida de los Mártires. All young patriots have faces full of asphalt.

*

"I have a cousin," someone tells me, "who's named Usnavy." A pretty name, I say—to say something. "Usnavy," he repeats. Yes, very pretty, I again reply. Seeing that I'm not getting it, he adds, "Like the US Navy."

*

At night, our car crosses the Avenida de los Poetas in the dark. I'm about to ask why the street has such a lyrical name when the rest of the car's occupants simultaneously tell me, "Lock your door."

*

"Who are you? What do you want?" the voice on the other side of the telephone demands again. I already told you, I respond, I'm Andrés. I was given this phone number, I've come to . . . for a novel. "Oh, now I understand, sorry!" The voice on the other side of the line relaxes. "It's just that here people steal cell phones all the time. And then they have the nerve to pick up your calls."

*

"Yes, yes, it's true," a friend confirms. "Last month my cell phone was also stolen. I called my number and the guy answered and started talking to me. 'Thief, you're a thief!' I yelled at him. He got really offended and said to me, 'What's your problem! Stop insulting me.'"

*

I browse some travel guides at the bookstore. I ask, out of curiosity, what sells the best. New York? Rome? Paris? London? "Denmark and

Turkey," the saleswoman responds. Noting my look of confusion, she adds with a smile, "This is Panama."

*

I stop at the small bookcase dedicated to Panamanian literature. I glance at a few consecrated authors: Gloria Guardia, Justo Arroyo, Rosa María Britton, Carlos Wynter Melo, Berna Burrell, Jorge Thomas. Books and names virtually unknown in Spain and Argentina, for example. The rest of the bookstore is filled with the same best-selling books that you see in the rest of the world. Far from being an intercultural exchange, globalization tends to give the big fish permission to swim in small ponds, too.

*

In an exaggeratedly Panamanian way, Rosa María Britton has lived in Panama, Cuba, Spain, and the United States. In *Todas íbamos a ser reinas*, a semiautobiographical novel about the transition from the Batista dictatorship to the Castro revolution, I read, "That summer I spent time rereading books in the personal library of my father, who was given to philosophers and such, and who would never have thought to buy a book like the Kamasutra."

*

We order a round of Balboa beer and crocodile tail. Young crocodile. The detail reassures me.

*

Panama is so obsessed with bridges, the very idea of bridges, that the famous Puente Centenario was inaugurated even before it was accessible. I'm told that people would drive out in their cars, park nearby, and cross a mud pit just to stand on the bridge. In Panama bridges bring sides into existence.

*

We eat in the Plaza Bolívar, in front of the place where the Amphictyonic Congress of Panama met at the behest of the liberator. "Nothing else," wrote Bolívar, "could fulfill the ardent desires of my heart." It was the first and perhaps only formal attempt to unite the Americas politically. In the old Franciscan convent, which currently serves as the Foreign Ministry, the room where the sessions took place has been preserved. Symptomatically, Bolívar decided not to attend the congress he himself had proposed. Today his statue presides over the plaza with a condor above it.

*

In Panama, invariably, everyone gives their opinion about the construction of the canal, as if commenting on a classic game or a controversial event. "The French," says a friend, "believed that one bank was higher than the other. How ridiculous! It was Panama itself that was going up and down. That's what the canal is, a watery stepping stone."

*

Panama, the crossing of crossings. Transit made identity.

*

"In this restaurant the dictionary changed," someone says, "or at least one word of it. We were having dinner with Vargas Llosa. It was the nineties. Suddenly a girl came through the door, recognized him, and went right up to him. She was a young, pretty white girl. He got ready to sign an autograph. But instead she asked him if it was true he was a member of the Real Academia Española. He nodded. Then the girl said, 'You should know that your dictionary says that *grajo* is the smell that black people have when they don't shower. I don't know how your armpits smell, but mine smell exactly like black people's.' Everyone at the table was silent. Vargas Llosa jotted something down in his notebook. We immediately changed the topic. When the next edition of the dictionary came out, the definition of *grajo* had changed."

*

I go to Chinatown with lofty expectations that are only partially satisfied. A few years ago, when the historic district was declared a World Heritage Site, most of the Chinese left the area due to legal restrictions. A few signs survive on the occasional storefront: "Spanish spoken here."

*

I read in the newspaper *Panamá América*, "The country fights not to be eliminated from the list of World Heritage Sites. It has until the end of the month to submit an emergency plan to UNESCO. . . . The Panamanian Society of Engineers and Architects warned that the historical sites . . . would be declared World Heritage in Danger, due to the lack of adequate measures for their protection." On the facing page, a Towerbank ad proclaims, "Some things should be extinguished."

*

Before going to the Canal Museum we stop at a supermarket to buy a turkey. The day after tomorrow is Thanksgiving. "Every year," my friend says, "I give the turkey a new name. Last year I called it Condie, for Condoleezza Rice. This year it's still nameless. Maybe I'll call it Carla Bruni."

*

Canal Museum. Exhibition on the construction period. Section: "Domestic Environment: The American Woman as Housewife." I read, "The Canal Commission made enormous efforts to bring American women to the Canal Zone. . . . Despite some critics' assertions that these women bored easily and tried to convince their husbands to return to the United States. . . . White married women, insofar as they played the roles of housewife and society dame, were considered a stabilizing force in Panama as in other colonial enclaves, reinforcing traditional values and what was deemed proper behavior."

*

The American feat was not so much technical (to go from a level canal to a floodgate system) as it was sanitary: to eradicate malaria and yellow fever transmitted by mosquitoes in the Canal Zone. These legendary insects had devastated the French, who left the canal in humiliation. Perhaps the *grandeur perdue* began in Panama, with the triumph of the little mosquitoes.

*

During the construction of the canal, twenty-two thousand men died. As much blood as water was spilled. "There are still people," whispers a friend, "who believe the canal should be a cemetery."

*

In a thousand years, the story of the construction of the canal will be the new version of the story of the construction of the pyramids. Slaves included.

*

In Guillermo Sánchez Borbón's *El ahogado*, to many minds the country's best contemporary novel, I read something that seems like a warning: "Something was left behind on the islands, stuck to the mountain vines, waiting in the swamps, ready to erupt tumultuously into the present. There is a great weight buried in the heart: something rotten flows through the bloodstream and populates our dreams."

*

Like a science-fiction novel with zombies, the American occupation left a colonial species for posterity: the suggestively and terrifyingly named *zonians*. That is, the occupants of the Canal Zone protected by the US Army and the zonian police.

*

The history of the canal is a blockbuster in four episodes, each a different genre. The first episode was an epic. The second, a war story. The third, a political thriller. The fourth, a folk drama.

*

Reading an article by Mariela Sagel, I learn that Gauguin traveled to Panama and wrote about it in his letters. I run to find a copy of *The Writings of a Savage*. The story is amazing. In April 1887,

Gauguin tells his wife about his exotic plans: "To recover my energy I'm going to Panama to live like a savage." And, referring to Taboga Island, he adds, "I know a little island in the Pacific, a league out to sea from Panama; it is almost uninhabited, free and fertile. . . . You needn't fear for my health, the air there is very healthy, and as for food, fish, and fruit, they are free." Barely a month later, the picture has changed radically. "Since the canal was dug," he writes, "these idiotic Colombians won't let you have a square meter of land for under six francs. . . . It's impossible to build yourself a hut and live on fruit; if you try they insult you and call you a thief." Although it seems unbelievable, Gauguin ends up being arrested for pissing in the street. "Because I had peed in some filthy hole filled with broken bottle ends and shit, they made me march through all of Panama. . . . I felt like doing something to the police, but here justice is expeditious: they follow you closely and if you move they shoot you in the head. Well, now the mistake has been made; it has to be corrected. I'm off into the isthmus tomorrow to wield a pick for the digging of the canal. . . . As for the death rate, it is not so frightening as it is made out to be in Europe; the black men who do the nasty work die at a rate of nine out of twelve, but the others die only half as often."

*

We drive along the sea on the Cinta Costera, a long beltway built only recently. "I'm scared of this road," says the driver, "the sea always recovers its territory."

*

"If the Panama isthmus didn't exist," someone claims at lunch in all seriousness, "the north of Europe would be uninhabited." Then

219

they speak of the warm currents, the oceanic transition between the Pacific and Atlantic, tectonic plates. But I remain fixated on this: the greatest power needs the smallest fissure to exist.

*

The canal captains are specially trained to cross the floodgates. Sometimes the giant ships have only a foot of separation from the banks. No foreign crew could do it. That's why when a vessel arrives, it waits in line, and, before crossing, the captain gives up his ship. The captain gives up his ship.

*

On the way to the canal, we pass by the Supreme Court. A flag hangs from the entrance with a legend below: "Praised be the Nation." For a split second, I see it wrong: "Pained be the Nation."

*

Finally, finally, we arrive. We go up to the lookout point. The ships descend little by little, sinking for the purpose of good.

*

A mix of physics and magic. To contemplate the functioning of the canal means to better understand water, its silent power, its fatal muscle. Water beyond national laws, a current that surges past those who wish to tame it.

*

First we see a Liberian freighter. Then a Greek oil liner. The latter, almost deserted, with its entrails open, occupied by only a few canal employees gathered at the prow, gives its warning in slow motion: "No smoking. Safety first."

*

Panama Canal. Souvenir shops. A nice transparent pen, which holds a small boat with bubbles inside, catches my eye. I look more closely: "© Aldeasa, Madrid, 2003."

*

In *El escapista y otras reapariciones*, a book of short stories by Carlos Wynter Melo, I find an Octavio Paz quote that defines imagination as the capacity to "see reality every day with the eyes of the first day." In this sense, traveling is a completely imaginary act.

*

At the beginning of the last century Panama became independent from Gran Colombia, to which it had belonged for over eighty years. I take out my wallet to pay for a drink. A few Panamanian friends immediately fix their eyes on the wallet. It's Colombian, I say. "It's Panamanian," they correct me, "from the Kuna Indians. Colombia appropriated their designs." I smile, pay for my Coke, and hide the wallet.

*

Fear, lots of fear, when I ride in the local cars. Driving is a constant save-yourself-if-you-can. Nobody uses lights or signals. Wherever, whenever, there are quick turns, shifts in direction, sudden crossings. The driver recognizes my panic, turns around, and explains, "I learned to drive during Noriega's dictatorship."

*

Yes, Panama is a permanently temporary place. For the first time in the entire trip, I don't need to go through security to leave the country. A single guard in the boarding area lazily takes my passport and simply looks for the entry stamp. "Go ahead," she murmurs, with the indifference of someone who no longer differentiates between those who are staying and those who are leaving.

*

"Have a good trip," says the gate agent. Have a good trip, I answer reflexively. Life is a canal.

San Salvador, Years of Tremors

"THE RUNWAY HERE IS VERY FLAT," a fellow passenger explains, "and it's easy to land. In Honduras it's different. The runway is short and it requires a lot of skill."

*

"Good evening," I hear an immigration officer say. "How are you?"
"Deaf," the passenger responds.

*

El Salvador has two main economic resources. The first, agriculture and livestock, has depreciated. The second, textiles, appears to be growing. This growth is due to the *maquilas*: immense textile factories built by multinational corporations that produce at an absurdly low cost. Thousands of workers, almost all young women, earn around 120 dollars per month. The country offers these corporations all sorts of tax incentives. Like capitalism itself, the maquilas operate twenty-four hours a day. I had heard of them before, but now, on the way to the hotel, I get an actual look at these instruments of systematic exploitation for the first time. I'm surprised to see that they're built so precariously, using only thin zinc walls. Despite the extreme heat, I'm told that there are no temperature controls inside the factories. And the government?

I naively ask. Can't they demand certain basic conditions? "If the government makes demands," they answer, "the maquilas just leave. They go to Nicaragua, Honduras, or Guatemala. And people lose their jobs." Aren't there human-rights inspections? "Sometimes there are. And when the inspectors come, the factories are already gone. Dismantled in the blink of an eye. That's why they're so sparse."

*

I stay in the department of La Libertad, twenty-five minutes from the sea and ten minutes from the mountains. "La Libertad," says the driver, "has many contrasts."

*

My hotel was built over archaeological ruins. An ancient indigenous Pipil settlement. Today the site is called Holiday Inn. It faces a McDonald's.

*

HOTEL IN SAN SALVADOR: Holiday Inn.
HOTEL ENVIRONMENT: Tense luxury.
RECEPTION STYLE: Furtive.

*

My chair moves. The table moves. The rooms, the walls, and the ceilings move. Objects tremble as if they had the shudders. Around me some people get scared, others laugh. "Welcome to the valley of hammocks," someone says, putting his hand on my shoulder, and then keeps on walking.

*

A few years ago, a triad of seismic tremors created an incredible symmetry. There were earthquakes on January 13, February 13, and March 13. The churches were filled until April 14.

*

Mauricio Funes, the new Salvadoran president elected after twenty years of conservative rule, was an investigative journalist. The Latin American left will undoubtedly have a better future with courageous reporters than with revolutionary military leaders.

*

President Funes advocates for a noncommunist left, and nonrevolutionary socialism. On the other hand, Vice President Sánchez Cerén, also the Minister of Education, recently endorsed a chavista manifesto in Caracas. Even without an earthquake, Funes's seat is starting to move.

*

"This is leftism light," complains a mature Chávez sympathizer, who apparently also belonged to El Salvador's guerrilla movement. And your leftism, I reply, is high in cholesterol.

*

The first time Mauricio Vicent interviewed her, Yoani Sánchez improvised an aphorism: "Life isn't elsewhere, in another place; it's in another Cuba." Today, two years later, he interviews her again and the aphorism progresses: "Reality is increasingly on the side of the opposition." A section of *Generación Y* talks about Internet restrictions on the island. Bloggers like Sánchez often manage their blogs without seeing them, sending posts to someone on the outside who uploads them onto the site. "Cubans," I read, "can't have a home Internet account. . . . I must send my blogs from hotels where the Internet charge is between seven and nine dollars an hour." That's why the blog accepts monetary donations in addition to connection hours in public places. To a certain degree that money is a clumsy subsidy to the Cuban government, which spurs the donations and legitimates Yoani Sánchez to ask for them.

*

"When I was young," says a friend, "I had many boyfriends with sweaty palms."

*

Night falls early. At this time of year, it starts to get dark at 5:30 p.m. There are cities that struggle toward the light of day, fearing the long night.

*

In the middle of that night, in Colonia San Benito, a police motorcycle, a bulletproof Toyota, and several black cars stop traffic and cross. "That's the President and the First Lady," says the driver. I ask the name of the street where we've stopped. "Avenida de La Revolución," he answers.

*

We have dinner in La Gran Vía mall. One of the few places where people (or more appropriately: the middle-class elite) walk freely and seem to burst with spontaneous joy. This is the unexpected function of commercial malls in countries like El Salvador. Not dehumanizing, but resocializing. On the basis of a certain per-capita income. Tonight *New Moon*, an adaptation of a novel in Stephenie Meyer's vampire series (the second? the fourth? the twentieth?), opens at the mall's movie theater. Here the last showtimes are usually at nine p.m. But for opening night the movie will be shown at midnight, on all screens simultaneously. Hours before they open the doors, the line of teenagers (and former teenagers) is already snaking around the plaza in front of the movie theater. Do commercial malls suck your blood? Depends on how you look at them.

*

We go through the wealthy Colonia Roma. The facades of the houses are striking. Or rather, the lack thereof: high walls crowned by electric wires loom in front of them. These private trenches were built during the 1970s. Then other earthquakes began.

*

The monument to the city's patron saint, Santo Salvador del Mundo (a little figure on top of the world, like a child standing on a beach ball), divides the city in two, just as great saviors tend to do. The partition is not a mystery. To the patron saint's right, toward the west, the residential, tourist, and executive zone. To the saint's left, to the east, reality.

*

Castillo Venturoso rises, inexplicably, on Avenida Roosevelt. In the middle of the twentieth century, the daughter of a rich landowner returned from Europe in the depths of melancholy. Apparently she had fallen in love with a certain castle. Her diligent father built her a replica to alleviate her pain. During the war, the family went into exile and the beautiful castle was left to its ghosts. Today it's a bank.

*

Parque Cuscatlán. Windy at dusk. I stop at the imposing monument dedicated to the victims of the massacres in El Salvador during the repression of the 1970s and the civil war in the 1980s. A Truth Commission, under the auspices of the United Nations, gathered testimonies. The number of the disappeared calls to mind my worst memories of Argentina: "Along with the thirty thousand names etched in this monument to memory and truth," I read, "there are many names that are not here because the victims were never identified. This space is dedicated to them, as a sign of respect and admiration. Their name is the homeland." Or their name rejects the homeland—what is done in its name.

*

Speaking of homelands. I reread the plaque and am surprised to find, just beneath it, an acknowledgment of gratitude to "the Spanish Association of Basque Conscientious Objectors for their donation to the etching of this plaque." A *Spanish* association? Of *Basque* conscientious objectors? We know that there were Basque separatists who fought with the guerrillas. Their name was also the homeland. But now they've been immortalized under the name of a very different homeland. The only unequivocal identity is that of these individual names, an interminable list, one by one: they are all dead. Their name is death. Everything else is publicity.

*

It takes your breath away, kills you a bit, to walk next to the long wall that invokes each victim's name chronologically. A hundred yards of death, arranged by year, from 1970 to 1992. Each year is split into two categories. One is "Homicides," the other "Disappeared." 1981 is the longest year: six plaques of death, ten yards of victims. The young driver who has taken me to the park admits that he's never before stopped to look at the monument. "That's my year," he says. "I was born in '81."

*

In Claudia Hernández's story "*Hechos de un buen ciudadano (I)*," the narrator is unfazed when he finds the body of a young woman in the kitchen of his house. Without any fanfare, he puts an ad in the paper to find the owner of the body. Several candidates call. Finally the character selects someone who was looking for a man. "I suggested that he accept the body that was in my kitchen," the narrator explains, "and present it to his family—in a closed coffin—as the relative they had lost. That way we'd be doing two favors: we'd be burying the girl and calming the man's relatives. He gladly accepted." Nothing disappears in reality without reappearing in fiction.

*

"That guy," they tell me the next day, referring to the driver born in 1981, "has a sad story." What is it? I ask. "His father and brother," they respond, "disappeared during the war."

*

Calle Rubén Darío and its surroundings, with its hundreds of mobile carts. Food, clothing, toys, CDs, cosmetics, bags, trinkets, decorations, furniture, sweets, electronic appliances: all contraband. I move through the hot mass of people. The corners smell of *pupusas*, corn or rice tortillas filled with cheese, beans, and pork rinds. It reminds me of a line by Rubén Darío: "Where pubescent young virgins offer you acanthus." "A dollar, a dollar!" the salesmen scream.

*

At the end of the street market, in front of the Plaza Central, rises the immense neoclassical structure of the National Palace. Statues of Isabel la Católica and Christopher Columbus flank the entrance. Gates now enclose the statues, because every time a demonstration occurred people destroyed them. "Last time," says a friend, "Columbus lost a hand."

*

"That," my friend points, "is the café where Roque Dalton used to go." It's called Bella Nápoles. I ask if we can go in. Its interior is modest: wood, white lights, and fans. The coffee is still served in *picheles*, aluminum jugs that conserve heat. Its history, however, is incredible. This place has always been the favorite meeting place for Salvadoran writers, artists, and intellectuals. Authors like Claribel Alegría and Ricardo Lindo Fuentes frequent the café. José Roberto Cea says that every morning for the last forty years he has arrived for breakfast at exactly 8:30 a.m. "This is where we, the old adolescents, come," he explains. This is also where, on July 11, 1980, they took away the young poet Jaime Suárez Quemain. The next day his body appeared with a slit throat. I find one of his poems online: "One day I will undoubtedly die / I will go with my rags somewhere else . . . / Without a single gesture or shout, / I drank the whole afternoon in one sip / and my tongue never remained silent."

*

National Theater of El Salvador. Weekly shows. Friday November 27 and Saturday November 28, at 4:00 p.m. Group: Los Sinverguenzas. Show: *Marx Has Returned*.

*

Our car ascends until we contemplate the nighttime panorama of the city, its lighting scattered due to emergency economic measures. Like drops of oil among the mountains. From up here, breaking with its custom, San Salvador relaxes. I ask what the place is called. "Balm Mountain Range," they tell me.

*

"When we were twenty," she says, "my friends and I were convinced that after having sex, we had to go back home with our legs closed tightly, so that nobody would notice that our hips had gotten bigger."

*

San Salvador airport. Check-in desk. A poet without knowing it, the guard says, "Sir, can you fill this form?"

*

From the window of the plane I see the dark-green squares of the fields, the blue dent of a lake among the folds of the mountain range.

With a mixture of knowingness and emotion, I think: It looks like Google Earth! This is the way things are. This is the way our eyes work. Bird's-eye images on screens don't evoke the feeling of being on planes. For us, it's the reverse: planes are like screens.

San José, Instructions for Getting Lost

AIRPORT IN GUADALAJARA, MEXICO. After a brief stop at the Guadalajara International Book Fair, where I don't do anything resembling sleep, I drag myself to the check-in counter to get the tickets for my final destination: San José, Costa Rica. I like, or maybe dislike, the sound of that phrase: the tickets for my final destination.

*

I can't find the customs form I filled out upon entering the country. This means a 262-peso fine, and, even worse, a date with the Mexican bureaucracy. I go to the police stand. The agent informs me that I must leave the terminal and pay the fee for the new form at a bank. I ask if I can't pay right here, and the agent responds that that's only possible for passengers arriving late. In other words, passengers who are on time receive extra punishment. I leave the terminal and walk to the bank. I wait in the appropriate line. When my turn comes, the bank employee tells me I can't pay with a credit card. Since I don't have cash, I must leave the office and find an ATM. I reluctantly obey, withdraw money, return to the line, pay the fee for the form, walk back to the terminal, and look for the same police booth. The agent asks for the paper, fills it out himself, and returns it stamped. At the bottom it reads, "Foreigner's signature."

That seems appropriate. I sign and say goodbye. When I'm boarding, the lost customs form appears inside the notebook in which
I'm scribbling these lines.

*

The Copa flight from Guadalajara to San José, with a stop in Panama,
becomes a small social laboratory for a silly reason: one of the plane's
bathrooms is out of service. This requires the passengers in coach to
invade first class, where a line grows steadily through the four rows
of premium seating. Both classes complain. The coach passengers
feel like they're intruding, and the first-class passengers feel like
they're no longer first class.

*

"When I was a year old," a Costa Rican passenger philosophizes,
"that year was one hundred percent of my time on earth. When I
was five, that year was only twenty percent. At twenty-five, only four
percent. And now, just imagine. That's why every year goes faster."

*

Flight from Panama to San José. Reality offers symmetries that
fiction would reject because they're too perfect. At the start of the
second part of the trip, I was on the same flight as the Uruguayan
Forlán, whose team was about to play Costa Rica. Today, on the
way to my last city, San José in Costa Rica, I'm sitting behind Pibe
Valderrama, a famous Colombian midfielder from my childhood.
Valderrama seems like an unshaven version of himself. Leathery
skin. Graying, scraggly beard. A dozen colored bracelets. A yellow
T-shirt with a small logo in the form of a fish, with the name Pibe

underneath. And his curly hair, now dyed with a golden tint that looks like a tribute to falsification. Valderrama amuses himself by doing crossword puzzles. There are pictures of celebrities around the horizontal and vertical lines. If he himself appeared, would he recognize himself? Would he get his name right?

*

Costa Rica has always had a reputation for being a hospitable and civilized country. Two details from the San José airport confirm this. In the immigration line, foreigners are referred to as "Visitors." And on one of the walls, for the first time in all of my travels, a sign explains exactly what the government does with its airport taxes. 12.15 pesos to Internal Revenue; 7.44 invested in the Technical Council of Civil Aviation; 5.41 for Airport Administration; and 1 to improve other airports in the country. Welcome to Costa Rica, Visitor.

*

HOTEL IN SAN JOSÉ: San José Palacio.
HOTEL ENVIRONMENT: Like a Ship in the Rain Forest.
RECEPTION STYLE: Distracted.

*

I stay in the Urraca neighborhood, one of the many green areas in the city. Trees, palms, and underbrush shine in the sunlight, and seem to blend with the wind. From the hotel window, in the middle of a gulley, I read, "For sale, approximately 5.5 acres."

*

"My friends used to call me Paco," a Spaniard tells me, "but here I prefer to be called Francisco. Since the Costa Ricans put 'Don' before everything, it sent chills up my spine when they called me Don Paco."

*

"The most elegant *ticos* call me *mae*," a friend explains. Spanish is a planet in the mouth.

*

Instead of dividing the international community, yesterday's elections in Honduras have reminded us who was on whose side. *El Mundo* reports, "The Foreign Minister, Miguel Ángel Moratinos, indicated that 'Spain doesn't recognize these elections, but neither do we ignore them.'" These are the unmistakable words of the minister. "From Tegucigalpa," *El Mundo* continues, "the Partido Popular's Member of the European Parliament, Carlos Iturgaiz, responded that . . . 'The elections were certified, clean, and transparent. . . . The position of Moratinos and the Spanish government will earn them nothing but international ridicule. Obama himself, Zapatero's guide in so many other things, left him with his ass hanging out this time.'" These are the unmistakable words of the PP. *El País* says something else: "Brazil heads a group of countries that refuse to accept the validity of the election. . . . Lula, who last week rejected Obama's request to recognize the legitimacy of the electoral process, did not make a statement." According to *El País*, Spain has proposed negotiating "a third way between the countries that negate any validity in an electoral process they believe to be the result of the coup . . . and those who defend the elections as legitimate and are eager to recognize the new government." *Público* summarizes this position by quoting the Costa Rican president: "Everything possible was done to revert the coup, which would have been a first in history, but it just wasn't possible. . . . We can't punish the Honduran people and make them suffer more than they've already suffered. . . . The worst thing would be to act with duplicitous morality. To accept results in Iran or Afghanistan, where we know the elections weren't clean, but not in Honduras. We can't turn the country into the Albania of Central America."

*

"With relish," they say, "*pura vida*," they repeat, "how rich," they celebrate. Such a hedonistic people must have suffered a lot. Here people smile at you and then take off.

*

"Here," she says, "there was lots of fighting so there wouldn't be a war."

*

Costa Rica does not currently have an army. Its national anthem doesn't boast of improbable epics or illustrious lineages. They limit themselves to singing: "Your children—simple workers—conquered / eternal prestige, esteem, and honor." And after a timid fighting verse, it ends by proclaiming, "Long live Work and Peace!" How do the other anthems I know end? The Argentine: "Let's swear with honor to die!" The Mexican: "To the resounding roar of the cannon." The Chilean: "Your noble, glorious standard / will see us fall in combat." The Colombian: "'Duty before life,' he wrote in flames." Suddenly the Spanish solution seems the most sensible: music without words.

*

Surprisingly, the presidential office is in Zapote, a middle-class neighborhood. I learn that the modest building used to belong to Fertica, a Central American fertilizer company. That explains everything.

*

In February there will be elections. "People will choose between the right and the far right," someone says. I ask about the left. "It buried itself," they respond. As usual. Why? "The PAC candidate acts like an evangelist. He's managed to scare away half of his voters."

*

One gets the sense that, despite the oceanic distance, Costa Rica is the Sweden of the Caribbean. Which entails a mixture of national pride and skepticism, calm and disillusionment. Costa Ricans tend to think that the country is getting worse, while the visitor feels that it's still a lot better off than many others. "One time," says a nostalgic voice, "one of my father's employees hit the president, who was riding on a bicycle by himself."

*

In San José the streets don't have names. And when they do, nobody pays attention. They also don't have street numbers. The ticos don't give directions: they tell you a story whose ending is your destination. I ask a friend for her address. She responds exactly like this: "Go up the traditional Escazú Highway until you get to the second bridge. On your left-hand side is the Riverside building, and in front there's a little road on your right-hand side. You take that road for one hundred yards and then one hundred longer ones, curving to the right. There there's a little guard post and a sign that says 'Dead End.' You go to the end, till you reach a black gate, and there you'll see another sign. My house is the last one; it's papaya colored. If I don't explain it like that, people get lost."

*

We get drinks at the bar Rayuela, which faces the Plaza de la Democracia. The ambience is incredible, the singer-songwriter horrible. The young poet Felipe Granados, who died a few months ago, used to come to this bar. He was thirty-three years old, exactly the age I'll be next month, when I return to Granada. Granados was HIV positive, and stopped treatment because it didn't seem to be working. "He came here to drink and think about who knows what," someone says. "He asked to be buried in a David Bowie T-shirt. For his wake his mother dressed him in a checkered shirt with a rosary."

*

I return to the hotel and look for information about Felipe Granados. He published only one book, *Soundtrack*. I find an endearing black-and-white picture of him. A handsome guy, with generous features, maybe gay, with a melancholic air it would be in bad taste to overinterpret. I find a text that Granados published last year in the magazine *SoHo*. It's called "The Last Day of My Life." Among its contents I read, "My last day should begin early, very early. . . . I don't want any ritual that leaves me in the hands of any known gods. I want them to know that I felt fine the day I killed God, slept like a baby, without any fears of hell or that other great abyss they call heaven. . . . I cry, I cry, but I still do things, while I shower, while I shave, while I go through the miracle of putting on clean underwear for the last time. . . . To sit and talk with a stranger about nothing, about whatever he wants. . . . Not to give into the temptation to judge him, not feel better than anyone else. . . . Not to make peace with my enemies, not to pardon the crimes done against me, not to blackmail the great beast of my guilt." If the moment of death is one of absolute lucidity, then Granados was prepared.

*

We drive by La Sabana, a gigantic park where the old El Coco airport used to be. That's where Kennedy landed during his only visit to the country, during the government of José Orlich Bolmarcich. I ask why JFK came. "To breathe in ash," the driver answers, who's been silent up to this point. "The Irazú Volcano," he adds, "had just erupted. He came to breathe in ash." Months later Kennedy was assassinated.

*

In *La Nación*, the most important newspaper in the country, I read an unbelievable article by the lawyer Ricardo Guardia, whose last name confirms that he was the one who drew up the first arms law in Costa Rica. "It continues to amaze me," Señor Guardia argues, "that it's not clear to some people that human beings rather than inanimate objects commit crimes." By "inanimate objects," Guardia means pistols, not the corpses that they produce. "When gun restrictions were introduced in Australia," he continues to enlighten us, "armed robberies increased by 51 percent and other violent crimes grew in similar proportions, due to the certainty among criminals that they were attacking defenseless citizens." One might extrapolate that in order to reduce violence, it would be better to have a shootout than to improve education and wealth distribution. Prohibiting the possession of arms, Señor Guardia reasons, would convert "thousands and thousands of honest Costa Ricans with firearms into criminals," in addition to "violating Article Twenty-One of the Constitution, which guarantees the right to life, by impeding legitimate defense." Is the Costa Rican state itself in violation of the constitution, since it lacks an army? Is this peaceful country violating the human rights of those who honestly know how to fire weapons? "Pura vida, Señor Guardia!"

*

I read in a story in Warren Ulloa's *Finales aparentes*, "Another controversy arose which took on the feel of a crime drama. The authorities catalogued the resurrected as having suspicious skin. . . . It was a kind of inverted genocide."

*

I walk, I finally walk, through the Avenida Central, a crowded pedestrian street full of popular shops. The store signs catch my attention. The smaller and more unobtrusive the sign, the more bombastic the name: Magical World, Grand Prix, Boulevard Style, Extremes, Energy. The shoe store is called Penny Lane. I pause in front of a sign held by a volunteer: "With art you can improve our children's self-esteem."

*

There are an extraordinary number of poets. To run into one poet is to meet a whole group of them. Poetry has always had this Masonic characteristic, which seems accentuated in San José. One of my favorite Argentine poets, Jorge Boccanera, lived in exile here. I find the Costa Rican edition of his poetry volume *Bestias en un hotel de paso* published by the extremely active Ediciones Perro Azul: "Place / is the name of the biggest animal on earth. . . . / Nobody moves here, it's the big day. / They divvy up the desert among all men." I browse in the bookstores Lehmann and International, flipping through books by local poets, who move interestingly between romanticism and colloquialism. In David Cruz's *Natación nocturna*, I read, "Destiny is a mask, / escape to the south like the birds." In Alfredo Trejos's *Arrullo para la noche tóxica*, "So many lonely streets / I carry under my arm." In *Verbo madre*, by Ana Istarú, "There's something, someone, like a sound that emerges. . . . / Listen: there is a small hand: it's putting down / the first mark of its story." In *Canciones cotidianas*, by the famous Jorge Debravo, "This city that we barely sustain / with the blood of those who still / haven't opened the husk of time." Or in Eugenio Redondo's *El columpio entre las hojas*, "It's not that God doesn't exist. / It's that he doesn't do commercials."

*

The Mercado Central, founded in 1880. Its sheet-metal roof and its ebullience remind me of my early childhood in the San Telmo Market. At the entrance, a panhandler with a Milan T-shirt scrunches his nose and spits. By his side a newspaper salesman enters, shouting, "They gave coffee with milk to the chicken! They gave coffee with milk to the chicken!" "Costa Rican bingo! Costa Rican bingo!" replies a lottery-ticket vendor.

*

Elevated, exposed flesh. An exaggeration of what they possess. Here the neckline doesn't lead down to cleavage, cleavage leads up to the neckline.

*

While I'm jotting down these notes, standing on Eighth Street, a parking attendant looks at me suspiciously. He asks me if I'm giving out fines.

*

I read the reversible edition of Luis Chaves's *Historias polaroid* (if you turn the copy around, like a magic trick, a second book appears). The brief poem "Coda" could serve as the slogan for this instantaneous book I'm writing, writing in movement: "Is it true? / That dipping one's toes in the ocean / is enough to understand its depths." I wish. But, when I invert the book of poems like an hourglass, the other book, *Asfalto*, warns me, "In the rearview mirror objects appear smaller than they actually are." What would happen if, traveling at full speed, one turned the rearview mirror forward? Would the not-yet-seen get bigger and bigger? Journeys are composed from "memories that go by like the electric-wire posts overhead." Writing is like the wires, the active energy that strings these posts together.

*

Lunch in the Teatro Nacional, a gorgeous neoclassical building that transports me from Central America to Central Europe. A friend tells me that during President Arias's administration, many buildings of historical significance are now in the hands of private multinational companies. Just before ordering a *crema de pejibaye*, I see a painting of the theater's facade with the caption "Not for sale."

*

While we're eating, we hear a *calipso*, music from the province of Limón. In Limón they speak Patuá, English mixed with Creole and Spanish. Suddenly I notice a water bottle on the table: "Limón Wuata."

*

I leave the Teatro Nacional for the Plaza de la Cultura. A rock concert by a young local group welcomes me. I stay and listen. They're amazing. Rock, sweet home, you'll always be with me.

*

I read an anthology of the new Costa Rican short story, *Historias de nunca acabar*. I like the title. The prologue by the authors Guillermo Barquero and Juan Murillo summarizes some contradictions of globalization, national identity, and virtual information: "We constantly use and debate the technology that allows for instant commentary on web pages about literature. . . . Yet still people read little, and, more importantly, know very little about contemporary national literature. . . . Books are cries sent into a public vacuum. . . . The adjective 'Costa Rican' that we put on the cover ends up being as arbitrary as any other marker. . . . These stories refuse to inhabit Costa Rica and, in most cases, move beyond national borders or move into the interior of an individual, far from the immediacy of this geographical space. . . . Amidst the distracting noises, we continue to hear the isolated shouts of those who try to resist the merciless accouterments of postmodernity with their voices."

*

On the last night, and I almost can't believe it's the last night, I toast the end of my journey with Imperial beer in a country without an army, and then I toast with Bavaria beer somewhere in the Caribbean, and then I look at the heavy sky of San José and ask myself where people go who no longer have anywhere to go. I think of the young poet Felipe Granados. I'd like for this to be his night, at least a little. And if he were to wake up, I'd like for him to have clean clothes to wear.

*

I listen to the first album by Malpaís, to many people's minds the best group of traditional fusion in Costa Rica. I read in the CD insert, "At the end of the Nicoya Peninsula, beyond Cabo Blanco . . . is the refuge of the displaced . . . the beach of basalt where we don't know if we're coming or going. The beaches of Mal País, Paraíso. . . . Perhaps as contradictory as the name of Costa Rica itself, for centuries the poorest place in the region."

*

I leave the room of my last hotel. I share the elevator with a man in a suit, who holds the door for me. For the first time in several months, I pronounce the word "gracias" with a clear, strong Spanish z. My body is moving toward the last airport. My mouth is one stop ahead.

*

San José airport. Immigration counter. "Destination?" the agent asks. San José, I sleepily respond. "In that case," she laughs, "I better not let you through, right?"

Writing Causes Travel

BEFORE I LEAVE, a friend tells me, "If you publish the notes you're writing, at some point you'll have to present them in every city that appears in the book." I imagine myself presenting the book in every place that appears in it and writing, at the same time, a journal about that second trip, which could be presented again, city by city, and so on to infinity. Once you start on a journey you can never quite end it.

*

A good portion of my life has been spent learning how to say goodbye. That could be the lesson of any life: giving all things the welcome they deserve, and wishing them farewell with the proper gratitude. From my first move as a child up to this day, I have said a series of goodbyes, some larger, some smaller. In this succession of farewells, whose intervals have been the very measure of my life, I can identify my transformations. Before, when I returned to my native county, I felt that I was saying goodbye to everyone. Now, I don't really know why, I feel like everyone else is saying goodbye to me. Maybe it's the effect of having gotten used to leaving. One loses the fear of having one's luggage dispersed, but also the certainty of owning its contents. Airports are the scenes of wrenching separations. And I realize that I have changed, so to speak, from the protagonist of my own goodbyes to a witness of other people's. The ways of leaving change as much as those who leave.

*

My second-to-last flight of the entire tour. Half of me feels the need to stop, to return home. Accustomed to the rhythms of travel, my other half tries to keep things going, to take me hostage. Maybe being permanently on the move is a secret method of staying put.

*

The feeling of having left something someplace. That we leave something everywhere we go, in addition to taking something with us.

*

We fly over the Spanish heartland. Beneath the plane the dry earth extends like an old sheet. We are the desert. Bedouins in search of an oasis. And we know that oases are often mirages.

*

Suddenly I don't need to fill out a single immigration form. Now my passport begins to blend with the place. Is that place the desert? Welcome to myself: this is also your country. I return to my other south and to my hard z's. I land with my accent, *aterrizzzzzzando*.

*

When I set foot in Spain, I remember my mother. My mother was a homeland.

*

Madrid, Barajas airport. Last plane, destination: Granada. When I board, I ask for permission to fly in the pilot's cabin. Many people have done it. I haven't. I think this could be a good end to the journal. An experience within experience. To fly within a flight. I ask, I beg. But no. They won't allow it. The captain approaches me affably and explains that since 9/11 it's no longer possible. "The problem," he adds enigmatically, "is the English." I imagine he means the Americans. "They're paranoid," says the captain, "you understand. It's psychotic. They report you. They report you and then take away your license. The English." I tell him thanks, not to worry. "Is there anything else I can do for you?" he asks. Yes, I answer, get me home safe and sound. The captain smiles and his eyelids tremble a little.

*

Flight from Madrid to Granada. I return to the reality of national unreality. In the seat next to me a Granada-born singer, Rosa, from the extremely popular talent contest Operación Triunfo, holds a bunch of flowers as yellow as her new bangs. As we land, she meticulously bites her nails. She is wearing sunglasses on a cloudy day. It looks like she hasn't slept.

*

Right before we land in Granada, my Granada, I try to translate the clouds we move through. In what dialect will I talk to my family when I hug them? Will I use *tú* or *vos*? *Ustedes* or *vosotros*? Will I call my love *sielo* or *cielo*? Landing is a doubt as high as taking off.

*

When the plane shakes, O temporary business class, all of the seats are gray in the dark.

*

A flight is made up of expectations, stations of the cross, supplications, miracles, and resurrections.

*

From my window I observe the hard, leathery skin of the Sierra Nevada. Below, solid, the land thinks. A wind turbine turns on a hill. In the seatback in front of me, the most recent issue of *Leer* magazine sports an energy ad that quotes a line by Sancho Panza about windmills. Below, the caption: "Literature, a source of energy." And a means of transportation.

*

Reviewing these notes, I realize just how many of them are things I heard, intuited, and read. And these second-degree insights flowed in part from our contemporary modes of communication. The Aymaras were right after all. Maybe they anticipated the future. Maybe today, more than ever, we should say, "They say that I have seen."

*

I don't believe that I've written what I've seen in this book. It would be more appropriate to say that I observed what I did because I was writing this book. A journal supposedly reflects our thoughts, experiences, and emotions. Not at all. It creates them. If we didn't write, reality would disappear from our minds. Our eyes would remain empty.

*

I haven't told the story of my journey in this journal. The journey has *taken place here*. The journal produced it.

*

One takes off to land in oneself.

*

I don't know who, how, where I am. Maybe that identity is more real than the others.

*

Does traveling quickly mean going through or around things?

*

Until the nineteenth century, the adventure of travel emerged from the fact of movement, from the vicissitudes of transportation. As Kavafis knew, Ithaca was traveling to Ithaca. In the twentieth century, with its ever-faster cars and ever-more-touristic planes, we became aware that movement itself was the least of our concerns. That the journey began once we arrived at our destination. Lately we have again become conscious of the work that displacement implies: airport chaos, luggage loss, fake agencies, station attacks, highway accidents, canceled reservations. They say the world is small. But small things can exist in many forms. We all have our own little worlds. Which can travel in our pockets, along with a notebook.

*

Hypothetically, globalization is always available. We don't really care to learn about a place until we go there. To be there and to know: synergy.

*

It's often said that nostalgia arises in the person who leaves, someone who remembers a place they've left. In reality nostalgia is the opposite. When we travel there's barely any time for remembering. Our eyes are full. Our muscles tired. And we use our remaining energy to keep moving. Packing suitcases forces us to suspend the past. Time slides off the skin of the traveler. For the sedentary person, on the other hand, time passes slowly and leaves a mark. Slowness is the motor of memory. Nostalgia comes to those who stay. There is nothing that makes us more pensive than going to the station to say goodbye to someone else, watching a vehicle get smaller in the distance and then disappear. Which of the two disappears?

*

Perhaps the greatest travel book, the most unpredictable of all, would be written by someone who doesn't go anywhere and simply imagines their possible movements. Facing a window that seems like a platform, the author would lift their head and feel the rush of the horizon.

*

Okay, I'm here now. But where is here?

JUNE–DECEMBER, 2009

ABOUT THE AUTHOR

ANDRÉS NEUMAN (1977) was born in Buenos Aires, Argentina, where he spent his childhood. The son of Argentine émigré musicians, he lives in Granada, Spain. He has a degree in Spanish Philology from the University of Granada, where he taught Latin American literature. He was selected as one of *Granta*'s Best of Young Spanish-Language Novelists and was included on the Bogotá39 list. He is the author of numerous novels, short stories, poems, aphorisms, and travel books. His first novel translated into English, *Traveler of the Century* (FSG), won the Alfaguara Prize and the National Critics Prize, and was selected among the books of the year by *El País*, *El Mundo*, *The Guardian*, *The Independent*, and *The Financial Times*; it was also shortlisted for the International IMPAC Dublin Literary Award and received a Special Commendation from the jury of the Independent Foreign Fiction Prize. His second novel translated into English, *Talking to Ourselves* (FSG), was longlisted for the International IMPAC Dublin Literary Award and for the Best Translated Book Award, shortlisted for the Oxford-Weidenfeld Translation Prize, and selected as the first among the twenty top books of the year by *Typographical Era*. His most recent book in English is the collection of short stories *The Things We Don't Do* (Open Letter). His works have been translated into twenty-two languages.

ABOUT THE TRANSLATOR

JEFFREY LAWRENCE received his PhD in Comparative Literature from Princeton University and is currently a professor of English at Rutgers University.

RESTLESS BOOKS is an independent publisher for readers and writers in search of new destinations, experiences, and perspectives. From Asia to the Americas, from Tehran to Tel Aviv, we deliver stories of discovery, adventure, dislocation, and transformation.

Our readers are passionate about other cultures and other languages. Restless is committed to bringing out the best of international literature—fiction, journalism, memoirs, poetry, travel writing, illustrated books, and more—that reflects the restlessness of our multiform lives.

Visit us at www.restlessbooks.com.